CHRIST IN Y'ALL

CHRIST IN Y'ALL:

Following Jesus into Community

_____

By Neil Carter

Ekklesia Press

CHRIST IN Y'ALL
Copyright © 2008 by Neil Carter
ISBN 978-0-9765222-7-0
LCCN 2008-934693

Ekklesia Press is an extension of www.kingdomcitizenship.org

Printed in the United States of America.

To April
my intimate ally, closest friend, and wife

And to the brothers and sisters with whom we meet
in Lithia Springs. I thank God for your love and passion.

Acknowledgments

First of all, I must acknowledge those whose previous writings and ministries have influenced me over the years, ultimately making this book possible in their own ways. I owe a debt of gratitude to writers I have known, such as Gene Edwards, Frank Viola, and Jon Zens. They in turn were certainly helped by other significant figures like Watchman Nee, T. Austin-Sparks, F.F. Bruce, and too many others to name. I have also personally benefitted so much from the ministries of Gene Edwards and Tim Richey that I will always thank God for my time with them.

Many thanks go out to those who have read manuscripts for me: Cindy Stallings, Jerry Mayo, Jon Slusser, and Mike Morrell. Thanks also go to Tim Price for helping me navigate the maze of details that go along with self publication. Over and above that, I am grateful to Jon Zens for making numerous editorial suggestions, as well as for encouraging me to put this volume into print. And finally, to my wife, April, I am ever grateful for her patience with the writing process, and for her lending her exceptional literary sense and skills to this project.

Contents

Author's Note

You hold in your hand the product of nearly twenty years of searching. I have tried to squeeze into these few pages the most important discovery I have made along the way: that the Christian life was meant to be lived out in community.

I believe the gospel itself inexorably leads to being *with* other believers. Following Jesus means encountering scores of other folks who are also following him. Yet we have somehow managed to assemble ourselves in ways that inhibit our connectedness. We worship alone, even in a crowd.

This book attempts to show that the gospel affects more than just the afterlife, calling Christians to know and love one another now, like a real family. The Savior and Lord of all creation has seen fit to gamble his reputation on this very thing. We must learn, then, what it means to be called children of God, brothers and sisters to one another.

I have borrowed heavily from people whose writings have influenced me most: Watchman Nee, T. Austin-Sparks, Norman Grubb, Gene Edwards and Frank Viola to name a few. Hopefully you will find here not a mere repetition of the things they say, but my own retelling of the things I have internalized and made my own. They originally put into words what my own heart was trying to say, and I am forever grateful to them for that. Now it's my turn to take what little bits I have seen and offer them back to the Body of Christ in hopes that they will become food for someone else.

You may find parts of this book challenging, especially when I question the necessity of things like church buildings, pews, paid staff members, Sunday School, and even the Sunday morning sermon. I should clarify that I believe these things help many people. If you are one of those people who are happy in a traditional church environment, I ask that you not be too greatly troubled by the thought that others like me feel led down a road less traveled. I'm not convinced that all Christians are meant to embark on this journey that I've begun. But I do believe that every follower of Jesus could use a fresh re-examination of the gospel itself. We already know the good news to some degree, but *there's more*. I think there always will be.

So in the spirit of reaching ever higher, I offer these pages for you to consider. I hope they kindle in you a flame that will only grow in time.

Introduction:

A Living Room for a Sanctuary

After several minutes of quiet conversation with God, I open my eyes and remember that I'm sitting in my neighbor's living room with about 25 other people that I hardly knew just a few years ago. These people, many of whom moved here from other parts of the country to be together, have become closer than family to me. Together we have weathered fierce storms, both literal and figurative. We have also touched places of spiritual depth and reality that I think most Christians don't even know they're missing. Somehow after these few-but-full years I feel like I've known these people my entire life.

We are very different from one another. I doubt that any of us would have naturally chosen each other as brothers and sisters in this community. We've got former Baptists, Lutherans, Episcopalians, charismatics, Evangelical Free Churchers, and

Calvary Chapel folks as well. We are an electrical engineer, a computer programmer, a physical therapist, a builder, a teacher, a photographer, a maintenance technician, a waitress, and a stay-at-home mom. We've come from different states, different cultural backgrounds, and we have vastly different spiritual histories. If you were to ask each of us our views on politics, education, or eschatology, you'd get about as many different answers as there are people in the room. Somehow this has never been a problem for us. Thinking alike has never been our goal anyway.

We do not have a special name for ourselves. We don't have any special buildings for our meetings. We don't have a pastor or a ministerial staff to support. And we lead our own meetings. We write many of our own songs (then we "borrow" the rest from other people!). We meet in one another's homes, and we try to live close enough to one another that we can walk to each other's houses. Because of our proximity to one another, we get to see each other often. We frequently eat meals together and watch each other's children. Our kids play together almost every day. We're a pretty tightly-knit community. The longer I live here, the harder it gets to imagine wanting to live any other way.

Folks looking in from the outside call us a "house church." If they'd look a bit closer they would see that we are so much more than that. We are a family, bound together by invisible cords that will not be broken by anything short of the Divine will itself. We meet with one another, living within two or three blocks of one another, because we have each come to see the community of believers as the best context in which the life of Christ can freely grow and thrive in us.

Let the Word of Christ Dwell Richly

People often say that they would give anything just to hear God's voice clearly. If only he would speak to them, then they could really relate to him and know him better. Sometimes I forget that I used to yearn to hear him speak to me, too. I forget because hearing him speak has become as natural and normal to me as putting on my clothes in the morning. How is that possible, you may ask? It's simple, really. I live in the midst of a group of people who know that they are the body of Christ because Christ lives inside of them. They know that his presence fills their lives and permeates the room when we gather together. They know that they speak on his behalf, for that is what it means to speak in his name. *They have been authorized to give voice to the motions of his Spirit within them.* They will not sit idly by, waiting for someone more qualified to come along and speak for them.

As I look around the room, I see evidence of the living presence of Jesus in my day. Sure, they're nothing exceptional on the outside. But on the inside, they are carrying the most valuable riches this world has ever seen. For this reason, these are the most beautiful people in the world to me. When they open their mouths to speak, I listen with the full expectation that the Spirit of Jesus will once again make himself known in this gathering of simple believers.

Incidentally, I have virtually no special place in the

meeting. That's really worth noting since I am the only one in the room with a seminary degree. In a place like this, a theological education just isn't as necessary as you might think. All those Latin phrases and philosophical categories for truth that I learned can't hold a candle to the palpable presence of the Holy Spirit. These people don't need me to guide their doctrinal development. That anointing that John told us about is doing the job quite nicely.

This should strike you as significant coming from a guy who once intended to be a pastor. I was once well on my way, years ago. Just a few days after I began following Jesus, I was asked to share my story in front of about 200 of my peers. I loved doing it, and they loved it, too, because it was a dramatic story. I was 16 years old, and I had something like a "Damascus Road" experience. The turnaround for me was so prominent that several of the leaders of my youth group later told me it took a while for them to really trust that I was for real. The next time I gave my testimony it was in front of 2000 of my peers. It seemed to me at the time that I was meant for great things.

So how did I end up in a living room with 25 people, among whom I have no special place? That's essentially what this book is about.

This Ain't Your Grandmother's Church

If you've been paying attention lately, you've noticed that a growing number of people are forsaking traditional brick-and-mortar churches for something else. George Barna estimates that as many as 20 million Americans will attend a house church meeting in a typical week.[1] At the same time, over the last decade average attendance at traditional church services (excluding megachurches) has dropped by 13%.[2]

My church family and I are not alone in our non-conformity. A casual stroll through the shelves at Borders or Barnes and Noble will reveal a seismic shift toward experimentation when it comes to "doing church." These folks are not simply dropping out of church or falling away from the Christian faith. On the contrary, they are actively looking for new ways to practice being a follower of Jesus in a world where pipe organs and pews no longer make much sense.

If you ask these folks why they are doing what they are doing, you may hear any one or more of the following:

- *My church was too impersonal.* Hundreds of people file into the same building for an hour or two only to drive back home without a single meaningful conversation with another person. Besides that, every six or seven years the faces are all different—including the ministers!
- *I got burned out.* Every time I turned around my church was introducing a new program or emphasis, complete with sign up sheets, t-shirts, and a color brochure. My family and I ran ourselves ragged trying to keep up with all of our obligations, hardly leaving any time to be together as a family.
- *Boredom with the ritual.* Same thing every week. Same ancient songs sung by ancient people. Same unanswered invitation given every week, no matter what the subject of the sermon. Come to think of it,

---

[1] http://www.barna.org/FlexPage.aspx?Page=BarnaUpdate&BarnaUpdate ID=241

[2] http://www.religioustolerance.org/chr_tren.htm

wasn't that the same sermon we heard about this time last year?

- *Abuse at the hands of another believer.* Brother Bob called me into his office and made it clear that my questions were unwelcome. Or maybe the "in" crowd at my church made it clear that I was "out" whether I realized it or not.

- *They don't seem to care about anyone but themselves.* No social conscience at all. All they seem to care about or sing about is getting into heaven when they die. What happens until then? Shouldn't we have some kind of impact on the world around us in the meantime?

These are just a few of the most common reasons why so many people are leaving the traditional church setting for newer territory. Incidentally, I wish I could tell you that they are all finding new expressions of the Christian faith where all these shortcomings disappear. But anyone who has lived long enough knows that human nature doesn't change with a change of address or vocabulary. Problems like this will surface no matter where you go. Because of this, you will need a deep and far-reaching vision of why we are here, and what we are about.

The Bible Made Me Do It

As for me, I left traditional church for a different reason. My journey began with *a rediscovery of the gospel itself.* I didn't leave for cultural or social reasons. I didn't leave because anyone was mean to me. I didn't leave because I didn't fit in. In fact, I think I fit in pretty well (at first, anyway). But then I did what everyone kept saying we should do: I read the New Testament.

I don't mean that I read a chapter a day, or that I read lots of random passages arranged according to topic. I mean I read it like it was a story, with real people talking about real things that were happening. That can be very dangerous, by the way. If you set out to do that you will eventually deal with the fact that their lives and our lives do not quite match up. They had a message and an experience that looks nothing like ours today.

Some of those differences can't be helped. They lived in a premodern Roman Empire, while we live in post-industrial cities and suburbs. They traveled on foot. We use planes, trains, and automobiles. They were hearing the name of Jesus for the first time. We were born into a post-Christian world, already saturated with the symbols and vocabulary of centuries of Christian history. All of these differences force us to accept a certain amount of discontinuity between the first-century believers and ourselves. As Rob Bell pointed out, "The goal is not to be a 'New Testament church'. That makes the New Testament church the authority."[3]

But some things transcend cultural differences. Contexts change, but the gospel itself does not. The questions that we ask may be new; but the centrality of Christ in the answers will always be the same, no matter what our circumstances. In my journey through the scriptures I encountered elements of

---

[3] Rob Bell, *Velvet Elvis* (Grand Rapids: Zondervan, 2005), p.65

following Jesus which do not have an expiration date. I found a gospel that impacts more than just me and my own personal future. What I read and what I experienced merged together to reveal that God's Spirit is always seeking ways to express who he is, right now, in this life.

In order to do this, God often leads his people into unexpected places. He often provokes us to let go of familiar things so that we may know more of his grace and mercy. For this reason, I find myself yoked together with an unlikely community of people. Each of us has left the beaten path because we followed the leadership of God's Spirit, and this is where he brought us. Each of us could tell a different story about how we came to be here, but you will notice common threads woven through each one.

Some here have gory tales to tell about their traditional church experience, but that's ultimately not why they're here. They're here, as I am, because they were drawn by *good news*. Somewhere along the way they encountered a Christ who is bigger than our own little minds could think up. They have found a Savior who will not be domesticated by anyone's culture or traditions. I want to tell you more about this Savior; but first let's look at what we passed up in order to lay hold of him. Let us consider for a moment our "half-baked gospel."

Chapter One:
A Half-Baked Gospel

Surely you have taken part in a workshop or a training session of some sort in which you were taught how to share your faith. Sometimes they use a tract. Sometimes they teach with an audio-visual presentation or a skit. Whatever the format, the gospel is always boiled down to a handful of statements that people are supposed to grasp. You know the points:

- God loves you and has a plan for your life.
- He wants a loving relationship with you, but all of mankind has turned their backs on him in disobedience.
- Now sin separates you from God and you will die without him unless something changes.
- Jesus came along and lived a sinless life and died on a cross in order to receive in himself the penalty for your

sins.

- God raised him up on the third day and now he stands at the door of your heart and knocks, so that if you will only ask him into your heart then you will be with him in heaven when you die.

Sound familiar? Of course it does! Much of it sounds like the beginning of Romans, with a verse or two thrown in from somewhere else. Maybe you learned *The Romans Road to Salvation*. Maybe it was *The Four Spiritual Laws*, or *The Answer Tract*. I remember when someone taught me how to cut up a piece of paper while telling the story so that when I finished it spelled "Jesus," with a paper cross left over. Maybe you made a bracelet with colored beads that each stood for a different point in this presentation. These have all been effective tools for many in learning to share their faith with people whom they ordinarily wouldn't gather the nerve to address. Don't misunderstand me—I'm not saying that these things are all bad. I have seen how God can be very skillful in using even *silly* things to bring us to himself (remember Balaam's donkey?). He knows those whom are his, and he will win them through whatever means are necessary.

But there are some major flaws with this entire approach. For starters, we still seem to be operating under the impression that becoming a Christian is a matter of learning a four- or five-item recipe for how to be saved. In other words, we define a Christian as someone *who believes the right things about justification by faith.* Many evangelical Christians believe that

Catholics aren't "saved" because they have a "works righteousness" mentality. It is evident that the watershed issue for these evangelicals is whether or not one *thinks correctly* about salvation. As Stan Grenz points out, "Our goal in proclaiming the gospel should not merely be to bring others to affirm a list of correct propositions."[4] Incidentally, squeezing the gospel into a propositional form like this will not do much for an increasingly postmodern culture. Many who are coming of age in the information age will feel that there's something smug about these neat little "bulleted" points in our presentation. I believe their distaste is justified (I will discuss what I believe can be done about it in Chapter Eleven).

Another major problem with this kind of evangelism is that it too easily divorces faith from a real relationship with God. Our "converts" are left with the impression that if they will only say these right things, pray this right prayer, and agree with these right principles, then they've got it covered. How many millions of people since the revivalist period of the mid-to-late 1800s lived their lives essentially alienated from any vital relationship to Christ or the Church because of this tiny gospel? How many have lived under the delusion that, since they remember a specific time in their lives when they "prayed the prayer to receive Christ," or went forward during an "altar call," then they are true followers of Jesus?

---

[4] Stanley Grenz, *A Primer on Postmodernism* (Grand Rapids: Eerdmans, 1996), p.171. See also N.T. Wright, *What St. Paul Really Said* (Grand Rapids: Eerdmans, 1997), p.159.

The well-known "once saved always saved" formula fails to recognize that true faith will endure throughout the changes and stages of a person's life. Faith worth noticing will produce the recognizable fruit of the Spirit long after that person has "walked the aisle." Those evangelicals who rail the hardest against the language of "works righteousness" are ironically the same ones who put the most stress on knowing a specific time in your life when you "asked Jesus into your heart." They seem to believe that this is the one remaining "work" required for salvation. For them, it all comes down to whether or not you did this one thing. But real faith in Christ leads to a lifetime of knowing and following him.

It's All About Me

A third problem with our presentation of the gospel (or what we know of it!) is that it's centered on us. I remember being taught to ask: "If you were to die tonight and appear before God, and if he were to ask you why he should let you into heaven, what would you say?" It was a novel idea when this approach was first thought up. Perhaps it was even effective for some purposes. But what message are we trying to send? Is this what we think being a Christian is about? If we choose this as our starting point, we may never rise above our own egocentrism.

Jesus came into the world to introduce something new: a kind of self-giving love that the world did not recognize. His every word and deed exposed the selfish aims of the fallen human heart. He made it clear that his presence among us signaled the inauguration of a kingdom that, effective immediately, will last forever. But when we tell the story of his coming, we couch it in terms of "fire insurance" for you that will kick in when you die. This will never confront the self-centered and individualistic habits of thought and lifestyle to which we are enslaved. We are only accommodating the self-interest inherent in everyone by offering a ticket to heaven for the low, low price of praying a special prayer. A.W. Tozer's words ring true:

> Faith may now be exercised without a jar to the moral life and without embarrassment to the Adamic ego. Christ may be 'received' without creating any special love for him in the soul of the receiver.[1]

Finally, because our grasp of the gospel is rooted in a thoroughly individualistic mindset, we are often setting people up for failure by giving them a churchless salvation. The life of faith wasn't designed to be lived out in solo. The risen and indwelling life of Christ is best experienced while living in a community of believers who know one another well. Together they can pursue intimacy with Christ in a simple but life-encompassing way.

I learned to present our gospel in a "hit and run" fashion, sharing the "plan of salvation" with someone I just met, knowing that I would likely never see him again. Evangelistic crusades and tent meetings share this same characteristic. They cast a wide net of mass evangelism (maybe even on television or

---

[1] A.W. Tozer, *The Pursuit of God* (Camp Hill: Christian Publications, 1982), p.12-13.

online) only to move on to the next town and a new crowd the following day. As a corrective, many evangelistic organizations make valiant efforts to connect newly converted believers with local churches.   Once they are there, however, they will probably not find a truly life-encompassing community that pursues authentic intimacy with Christ. Notice that I said that Christ is best experienced *while living in* a community such as this. The traditional congregational church model does not (or rather cannot) provide this kind of environment. It is structured in a manner that actually prevents authentic community from developing (more on that later).

In contrast to this, consider how Paul labored in a town until a community was established.   This community could nurture and develop these new believers for the rest of their lives.   He never simply preached the gospel to "get people saved." His goal was always to establish churches which would fully realize the purpose for which Christ came. He labored to build on this earth a house of living stones in which God himself would live and freely express his life-giving love.

So what are we missing? Simply put, we are missing *the rest of the good news*. The good news does not stop with our justification, our induction into heaven. Yes, it's true that Jesus died for our sins. But his death accomplished much more than that. We need not wait until we die to reap the benefits of the work of Christ! There are things that God intends to produce here and now, on this earth, which will blow your mind. As you move into a practical expression of those things, chances are also good that you'll find many of our religious traditions superfluous, leaving them behind.

The Rest of the Gospel

Jesus said that the "good news" was that the kingdom of God had come. In fact, it seems he couldn't stop talking about the kingdom — only he never defined what exactly that kingdom is. He kept telling stories, each one illustrating a different facet of kingdom life. He seemed determined to couch this great thing in mystery, never fully disclosing what it would look like or how it would come. We are led in the end to look to the epistles to discover what the kingdom of God signifies. What we find there, however, is that Paul exchanges the language of kingdom for that of a *new creation*. He speaks of a coming age in which all things are reconciled to God. And somehow, this new world becomes available to us here and now by God's indwelling Spirit.

His letter to the Romans lays out his gospel more completely than any other letter. Unfortunately, we "evangelicals" have failed to see that *the whole letter recounts his gospel*, not merely the first four chapters. When most of us try to answer the question, "What is the gospel?" we hit the highlights of only the first part of the letter, forgetting what follows after it. If we were to keep reading, we would learn that "While we were enemies we were reconciled to God through the death of his Son; how much more, having been reconciled, shall we be *saved by his life."* [2]

Saved by his life! I remember when these words first leapt off the page and caught my attention. My heart jumped and I thought, "You mean there's more?! Holy cow!" We have more to be saved from than just the final judgment. We have been quite focused upon the death of Jesus for our sins. Our gospel centers completely on that one thing. But there's something far more important than even that for us to discover. His death for our sins was not an end in itself. It was a means to an end. But what?

As a child of Adam, I have been enslaved to invisible forces so familiar to me by now that I scarcely realize how bad off I have been. Death has been working in me in such subtle ways that I have grown accustomed to its smell. I have been asked before, "Are you saved?" There are at least two answers to that question. Yes, I am saved. But then again, I'm still being saved even now. I'm not totally "saved" yet, and I won't be completely saved until this carcass that I carry around gets renewed by the sound of his voice. Until then, the saving life of Christ will have to continue working out this salvation, bearing more and more evidence of his redeeming presence as time goes on.

When God first created us, he intended to fill us with the same self-giving love that drives him. It is his very nature to share and to give his life for another, for God himself is a

---

[2] Rom.5:10

community (Father, Son, and Spirit). From the beginning, he desired to produce a vast family which would share his character and live as a community. For this to happen, his life would have to be placed *within* us because only his life has the capacity to truly love like this. So he designed us "in his image," much like the suit in my closet is designed in my image. It's made in just the right shape to fit me. Our Creator designed us to express who he is in a way that is unique among all other creatures.

But something happened that sidetracked his original intention (all within the larger confines of his sovereignty, mind you). We learn from the story of Eden that the human race has been infected by something which was never supposed to enter into us. We received the wrong spirit within us.[3] It is a spirit that takes the self as the center of all things, turning our energies and passions inward upon ourselves. In time, our lives became marked by a single-minded pursuit of self-promotion. Our hearts, which were originally designed to love and to give, mutated into engines of self-interest and egocentrism. Whether in pursuit of good or evil, one motive seems to undergird every activity of this human race: the promotion and preservation of the self. Thousands of years dominated by this self-serving spirit have warped the faculties of the human personality and have even ultimately marred the physical creation itself. This was not the world that God had in mind when he said, "It is good."

[3] Eph.2:2

The good news is that *a new reality has broken in through the death and resurrection of Jesus.* A new kind of life has appeared in him. It is not simply a life that is longer in duration, but a life that is of a different sort altogether. This kind of life has the power to end the silent tyranny of this self-serving yet self-consuming presence. Being "saved by his life" means that we are not merely forgiven of our sins; more than that, the risen life of Jesus comes to us as another kind of salvation – a salvation from ourselves!

God's purpose is not completed in creating us to only remove the penalty of our sins. In other words, he didn't create us just to save us. He was after something in the beginning that he didn't get. The good news is that he comes to us in his Son to finish what he started in the first place. He has come among us to establish his kingdom—to reproduce his righteousness in our very midst today! This goes way beyond a mere "ticket to heaven." How could we ever have settled for less?

Often Imitated . . .

A word of caution: I am not talking here of a mere "imitation of Christ." Jesus didn't come down to earth simply to show us the right way to live. That's too shallow a view of who he is. I am just beginning to learn that Christ himself *is* the entirety of my spiritual life. I don't have faith because I'm imitating Christ's faith; rather, I believe because he lives inside of me and *he believes.* His faith has become my faith. I don't love because I'm trying to live like Jesus. I love because *he is love* and he's living in my own heart now. That's the difference between imitating Christ and becoming indwelt by him! One makes me strain to become something that I'm not. The other leads me to discover who I have already become by his grace.

In the movie *Anastasia*, two Russian con artists discover a young girl and try to pass her off as the long-lost heiress to the throne. They teach her how to walk, talk, and bow like Anastasia. They fill her mind with the kinds of facts and trivia that the real Anastasia would know. They load her down with so many things to memorize that she almost decides to give up. Then one day she recalls a few details about Anastasia's life that neither of them ever taught her! They soon discover that she *is* the real Anastasia, and her grandmother recognizes her immediately. After all that pretending, it turns out to be true. Being Anastasia became the most natural and easy thing in the world.

That's what it means to be indwelt by this Man. Something happens to you that defies explanation. You begin to remember things you never thought you knew. You will hear the Lord speak of marvelous things, things almost too good to be true. But no matter how incredible his declarations, somehow you just know they're right. You may even lose your sense of time. Truths that should belong to eternity make their home in the here and now, even in your daily life. It'll be like Gonzo said in *The Muppet Movie*: "I've never been there but I know the way. I'm going to go back there someday."

We need our minds renewed by the rest of the gospel. Then we will be able to recognize the gentle, quiet resolve that has been deposited in our hearts through his Spirit. With our new eyes we will be able to see that his yoke is easy and his burden is light. We will also discover that this journey was not meant to be taken alone. No Israelite endured the wilderness or claimed the lush land of Canaan on his own. This adventure was meant to be a "corporate" pursuit—a collective endeavor. It's a job for a "we" rather than a "me."

Look a little longer, dig a little deeper, and you'll see that the good news keeps getting better and better. Do you know what it means to be "in him"? Keep reading to find out...

Chapter Two:
One with Christ

$$===============$$

One of my two older daughters brought up the subject of heaven one night at the dinner table. Beth, who was five at the time, suggested that it would take a really long time to get to heaven. She wondered out loud if you could get there in a spaceship. Anna, the six-year old, instinctively looked in my direction to see if I was going to comment on her suggestion (of course I was). I said that heaven is not so much a place as it is an invisible world right alongside the one we see. I suggested that if we could split open the world that we see around us, then that other world would appear right in front of us. Without skipping a beat, Anna responded, "Wouldn't it be cool if we could just step into that other world and, you know, live there?" I agreed. That girl's sharp as a tack.

I think that most believers picture Jesus way up in

heaven (which must be somewhere far, far away) with themselves "down here" on earth hoping to curry his favor by the things that they do for him. They read about how Jesus lived, or maybe some other biblical character (better watch which ones you pick!), resolving to act that way themselves. One of the first things I learned to ask as a new believer was "What would Jesus do?" It seemed at the time like a good thing to ask. Maybe for some people that works. Didn't for me, though. I always ended up picking whatever was the most uncomfortable thing to do at that moment, calling that "what Jesus would do." Somehow that seemed to be the same thing. I suppose that's only natural.

Paul said that our natural selves (*lit.* our *psyches*) cannot grasp the things of the spirit because they are only discerned by the spirit.[1] In order to perceive the things of God, we have to use eyes and ears that do not belong to our natural selves. Jesus said that a person cannot even see the kingdom of God unless something new is born into him.[2] That is the spirit of which I am speaking. Jesus said that this life is "from above." It is not originally from this world at all. It is from the other realm. Paul calls that realm "the heavenlies." For him, that is not some far off "place." This realm is as near as your very breath.

Being In Him

The risen Lord Jesus is not "up there" somewhere beyond the stars, looking down on us while we live our lives

[1] 1 Cor.2:14
[2] John 3:3

here on this little planet. He has come to make his home inside you and me.[3] We are not separate at all. In fact, according to Paul, we are as much "up there" as he is. If we maintain that Christ is in heaven, we must also see that we are with him there, too. Let's consider some of the things that have been declared about us:

- When we were dead in our transgressions, he made us alive together with Christ… and *raised us up with him,* and *seated us with him in the heavenlies* in Christ Jesus. (Eph.2:5-6)
- *Since you have been raised up with Christ*…Set your mind on the things above, not on things that are on the earth; for *you have died and your life is hidden with Christ in God.* (Col.3:1-3)

Notice that these things are presented as already established facts. Our life is tucked away inside Christ, who is seated at the right hand of God. That's the place of all power and authority, by the way. Wherever he is, there we are. That's what it means to be "in him." To illustrate what this means, let me tell you a story.

My grandmother once told me about how she almost was never born. Her father had married a beautiful girl named Katie, who had recently "bobbed her hair" like many of the other young ladies of her time. Her more reserved sister, Cloanna, would have none of that. She wore her hair in the longer, more traditional style that she had always known. One day while the three of them were rowing a boat across a popular

---

[3] John 14:23

swimming spot called "the Big Eddy," the boat rocked hard and Katie fell out. Cloanna dove in to save her sister even though she never learned how to swim. Robert didn't know how to swim either, so he stayed in the boat and began desperately feeling around the swirling muddy waters for the two sisters who had now both been sucked under. Almost falling in himself, Robert finally grasped hold of someone's hair and pulled her up by it. It was Cloanna. Because of her long hairstyle, she survived while her sister drowned that day. Robert later married Cloanna and raised a family, which included my grandmother. So in a way, I too was saved by a haircut (or the lack thereof).

How could I say that, since I hadn't been born yet? It's pretty simple. I was "in" her long before I was ever born. Come to think of it, hundreds, thousands, potentially millions of people were "in her" when she was pulled up out of a watery grave. Ultimately, whatever happened to her happened to all of us. We were all "saved" by her hair.

Being in Christ is kind of like that. Did Christ die once and for all? Then we died once and for all. Did he pass through a grave and into the heavens? Then so did we. Whatever happened to him also happened to us. We inherited sin from our human ancestors because we were in them when they fell. In the same way, we inherit righteousness from the Lord Jesus because we were in him when he conquered death and sin.

Is Christ righteous and holy? Then we are righteous and holy. In fact, the New Testament routinely calls us *saints*, which means "holy ones." Is Christ beloved of the Father? Then we are also accepted *in* the Beloved.[4] Is he at peace with his Father? Then we also have peace with God through our Lord Jesus Christ.[5] Now look to the future. Is he subjecting his enemies under his own feet? Then so will we. Is he coming in glory? Then so will we appear with him when he appears. "We may have confidence in the Day of Judgment because as he is, so are we in this world."[6] That's a pretty bold statement. It should produce some pretty bold people.

The Good Infection

Oneness with Christ means that we are not only "in him," but he is also *in us.* For Paul, the gospel hinges on this statement: "I am crucified with Christ; and I no longer live. It is Christ who lives in me."[7] Christ in us *is* the Christian life. Put differently, our faith is not some "thing" that we practice separately from him. It is rather his believing in us, his loving in us, his dying and rising again in us. When Paul says that we should work out our salvation with fear and trembling, he says that we can do this "because it is God who works in you, both to will and to do according to his good pleasure."[8] He does this through the indwelling Spirit of his Son. He has fulfilled the promise that he made through Ezekiel: "I will put my Spirit in them and cause them to walk in my statutes."[9] Through the

---

4 Eph. 1:6
5 Rom.5:1
6 1 Jn.4:17
7 Gal.2:20
8 Phil.2:13
9 Ezek.36:27

indwelling of his Spirit in us, God's new covenant produces in us what the old covenant was never capable of producing: the fruit of the other realm.

C.S. Lewis calls this "the good infection."[10] We do not gain his nature by merely following a pattern of right behavior we have carefully observed in order to become more like him. That would be like trying to change a dog into a person by dressing it like one and teaching it to walk on its hind legs.[11] His life is a different kind of life. It cannot really be copied by another kind of being. It can only become ours by "catching it" from him as he comes to dwell within us. In us, that life slowly grows and matures until branch and vine cannot be distinguished.

Do you know that his Spirit is in you? Paul asked the Corinthians this very question twice, first referring to them as a whole church, then later as individuals.[12] His point each time was to bring home the reality that Christ is in us. The Spirit that has been poured out into us[13] is the Spirit of Christ himself. We find this to be true in our own experience, don't we?

Having lived among a group of believers who can relate to one another without the superfluous trappings of the Sunday morning ritual, I can attest to his real presence among us. When believers live together and worship together in an atmosphere

---

[10] C.S. Lewis, *Mere Christianity* (New York: Macmillan, 1952), p.153.
[11] For a compelling discussion of this, see Gene Edwards, *The Highest Life* (Wheaton: Tyndale, 1993).
[12] 1 Cor.3:16, 6:19
[13] Rom.5:5

of freedom and authenticity, God tends to "show up." When the saints that I meet with gather together to seek God, we are drawn together by something supernatural, something larger than ourselves. We are bound by a love that is not of this natural world. That's his Spirit in us, making his presence known.

The Spirit of Sonship

"God has sent forth the Spirit of his Son into our hearts, crying "Abba, Father!"[14]   By this indwelling Spirit, our relationship to our Creator has changed from one of subservient subordination to one of privileged sonship. As it goes on to say, "You are no longer a slave but a son."

Remember how, in the movie *The Lion King*, the hyenas would shudder at the sound of the king's name? One of them would say "Mufasa!" and the others would get chills. His very mention struck fear into the hearts of his subjects. Almost immediately after that, a totally different scene played out in which Simba bounded into the king's den, demanding that the king wake up. Invading his father's personal space, the bold little cub pried Mufasa's eyelids open and glared at him, saying, "Dad! You promised!" What a different relationship he had from the hyenas! What a difference sonship makes! It wasn't that Simba didn't respect or even fear his father's wrath. Later on he demonstrated that well enough. But fear didn't dominate his interactions with his father all the time. Sometimes he

---

[14] Gal.4:6ff

approached the throne with the familiarity that only a son can know.

That is the kind of relationship that Jesus suggested when he taught us to pray "our Father." He was giving us permission to step into his identity, into his relationship with his Father. From now on we would approach our Father in Jesus' name. That doesn't mean that we attach the phrase "in Jesus' name" on the end of our petitions to God. It means we assume his identity of favored sonship when we approach God.

Do you remember how Jacob received his father's blessing? Under his mother's direction, he covered himself with the smell of wild game and his brother's clothes. He even covered his arms with fur so that he would feel more like his older brother Esau. He *clothed himself* with Esau. The illusion worked, and Isaac received Jacob as if he were his brother. Jacob stepped into Esau's identity for a moment, and received the blessing that rightly belonged to Esau.

In the same way, we have assumed the identity of our Savior. We have become the aroma of Christ to God in everything that we do.[15] We have become "clothed with Christ."[16] Do you realize what that means? We have stepped into him and he has become our new identity. To our Father, we smell like his Son! We feel like his Son! Only this time we are not usurpers—we are not playing a trick. We have been freely given the gift of Christ as our covering. Because of this, we receive the blessing that belongs to the beloved Son, in whom

---

[15] 2 Cor.2:15
[16] Gal.3:27

the Father is well pleased. When we listen to what God has to say to us as followers of Jesus, we feel his pleasure in his Son as our very own.

I no longer need to approach him as the person I have always been. I need not rehearse my shortcomings with him in order to deserve the fatted calf. I am in Christ and he is in me. As we come to realize this new identity, "we have confidence to enter the holy place." We can "draw near with a sincere heart in full assurance of faith"[17] because we know that we are "in him" and that he is "in us." He is our acceptance. He is our access to the Father.

I AM . . . What You Need

Paul also says that Christ is our wisdom, our righteousness, our sanctification, and our redemption.[18] Do you need wisdom? Wisdom is Jesus Christ. Do you need righteousness? He is our righteousness. Do you seek sanctification? It comes from being "lived in" by Jesus Christ.

The men who first followed him had such a hard time getting this idea. They would ask him for bread and he would reply "I AM the bread of heaven. Partake of me and you'll truly live." But they didn't get it. When Martha pleaded with him to raise Lazarus from the dead, he answered "I AM the resurrection and the life." But they still didn't quite get what he

---

[17] Heb.10:19,22
[18] 1 Cor.1:30

was saying. Finally, Thomas pleaded, "Just show us the way," and Jesus replied "I AM the way."[19]

Like them, we are always seeking what he can give us, because we want to be better people. We want him to "show us how" so that maybe we won't have to keep coming to him all the time! Wouldn't it be nice to not need him so much? But he made the nature of our relationship clear when he said, "I AM the vine and you are the branches... apart from me you can do nothing."[20] A branch draws life from the vine and cannot produce fruit in its absence. In the same way, we who are in him will never come to the end of our need for his presence.

Incidentally, how many things do you do, either on your own or within your church, that honestly could not be done without God's indwelling presence? Think a minute on that question before you answer. How many activities are planned and carried out that do not truly require his presence to work? One of the reasons I left traditional church was that I couldn't think of anything I did in church which would *absolutely require* his presence.

An intense youth evangelist named Dave Busby used to challenge young men in youth ministry with this question: If the Holy Spirit were to pack up and leave your church tomorrow morning, would anyone notice the difference? Would anything at all change? What does it say about us if our answers are "no" and "nothing"? How many habits and practices of our churches are carried out because of tradition rather than any up-

---

[19] John 14:5
[20] John 15:5

to-date leading of the Spirit? I believe a large number of those young men who heard Dave eventually left their traditional backgrounds, too. They "emerged" right out of their churches and now they are trying out new things. They aim to grab hold of that dependence for which their hearts ache. They have come to believe that we must not hold too tightly to our religious traditions, because they can so easily become a hindrance to following the voice of our true Shepherd.

Hearing with our "Inner Ear"

Having him "in us" means that we can hear that voice and know him when he speaks. In the synoptic gospels (Matthew, Mark, and Luke) Jesus often said, "He who has ears to hear, let him hear." In John's gospel he put it this way: "My sheep hear my voice and they follow me."[21] This happens because we have his Spirit inside, and we have his ears. When he speaks, we respond. It doesn't even require a great deal of thought. It was a major discovery for me when I realized that I often hear his voice and respond without even thinking about it. The best way I know to describe what I discovered is with a story from my college days.

The dormitory I lived in for all four years of college had community bathrooms. Do you know the kind I mean? All the showers were in the same big room, all the sinks shared one long counter top, and all the toilets were lined up along the opposite wall, separated by fiber glass stalls. The walls and the

---

[21] John 10:4,14

floor were covered with bathroom tiles so that every sound you made reverberated for several seconds. This, of course, inspired a lot of singing. One day I remember singing Elvis's "I Can't Help Falling in Love with You." I discovered that I could hit the exact frequency of the fiberglass stalls, making them vibrate with my voice. It was on the word "help," and when I sang that note the stalls all shook so that it sounded like a large truck was driving by outside. I had found the stalls' wavelength, and they shook.

Hearing God's voice is like that. Your spirit, which is now one with his Spirit, matches the "frequency" of God's own voice. When he speaks, everything inside you can't help but respond to his leading. It often doesn't even require analysis – you just follow. Maybe his voice comes in the conversation of a brother or a sister in Christ. Maybe it will show up in a song on the radio, in a line in a movie, or even in your own thoughts. Whatever the vehicle, the effect is the same: You *just know* that what was said was right. It's like something inside you rises up and binds itself to what you heard and you know that you must follow that word. It becomes a part of you and you *own* it. This is how you will find that you hear his voice. It seldom comes as a dramatic event. Many times his voice comes simply, disguised in the every day things; but you follow it, just the same. This is what his life in you usually looks like. He seldom "appears" in a dramatic flash of light in front of your eyes. That's not his usual way. Instead, he quietly works on you from the inside out, changing your desires to match his over time.

Don't get me wrong: Sometimes God speaks after a long period of seeking his heart on a matter. And when that time comes, his desires may even contradict your own. You will not always follow his leadership effortlessly—without some struggle, some wrestling with God. Other times, he seems to say nothing at all. At times he seems to leave our decisions up to us, using whatever he has already taught us as our only guide. Either way, his best work is very understated.

I think that some people are expecting to fall into some kind of trance when God speaks. They want God to undeniably manifest himself within them, like they're being possessed or something. But that's not how it happened with Jesus. Remember how he said, "I've been with you all this time and yet you haven't come to know me, Philip? He who has seen me has seen the Father."[22] I'm sure Philip was confused at that point. It didn't look or sound any different from his usual conversations with Jesus. But Jesus went on to explain it this way: "I am in the Father and the Father is in me. The words that I say to you I do not speak on my own initiative, but the Father living in me is doing his works."[23] The indwelling of his Father looked just like normal living.

Normal Living

It has always amazed me that people from Nazareth were shocked when Jesus finally announced who he was. He had lived and worked in that tiny village for thirty years. How

---

[22] John 14:9
[23] John 14:10

could they not have known that he was special? Didn't he have a special glow about him as he walked about town? Didn't he fill his days with mighty works of supernatural power? The sovereign Creator of the universe inhabited human form for three decades and nobody noticed?! How could that be?

It could only be because God's work in Christ all those years consisted of normal, everyday things. He filled his days playing with his cousins, obeying his parents, and making doorframes, roofs, and plows. He sat and talked with friends and family. He sang songs and told funny stories and slept and ate just like the rest of us. He had to learn the scriptures along with every other child of Abraham. He had to sit through countless misreadings of the Torah and feel his blood boil and his stomach turn as they got it all wrong. Simply put, he had to endure everything that you have to endure from day to day. But every moment was holy because the Father was there with him, experiencing it all.

It's the same way with Christ in us. We are in him and he is in us, which is just another way of saying that we are one with him. His living in and through us doesn't look exactly like what you'd expect. It mainly looks like you living your normal life. It looks like you going to work, cooking supper, taking care of your kids, or paying the bills. Was Christ's oneness with the Father limited only to moments of ministry? If it was, then the first thirty years of his life were wasted on so many mundane, everyday things for nothing. No, *his indwelling by his Father gave meaning and purpose to every moment of life.* In the same way, our lives have become holy things—sacraments in themselves—with the presence of God touching everything we do. "For me, to live is Christ."[24]

Having Christ for our life doesn't mean that we get glassy-eyed and speak with stylized accents. It looks like normal life, but with something extraordinary going on "under the hood." On the outside, your activities don't always change. But on the inside, his motivation becomes yours in such a subtle way that it hardly occurs to you that you are being led to do anything. Our evangelical churches have long been preoccupied with imitating Christ. As it turns out, he's been hiding here all along, doing *his imitation of us.* The life you're now living is his imitation of you, living your life as if nothing has changed. But deep down everything has changed. In hundreds of subtle ways, in your basic attitude and priorities, he is there. He may be disguised, but those who know his scent are not fooled.

Unfortunately, I do believe we have been fooled about one thing. Too often this "hiddenness" of the Spirit of Jesus gets overlooked, leading us to manufacture more deliberately religious kinds of experiences in pursuit of his presence. Each week, we put on our least comfortable clothes and file into special buildings in which we will speak and sing in a special way—totally removed from the style and manner of the rest of our daily lives. Why is that? Why must the way we act "in church" be so different from the rest of our lives? I suspect it is because we have failed to grasp that his life truly permeates all that we do. We need a heightened sense that Christ in us feels

---

[24] Phil. 1:21

at home in the mundane details of everyday life.

A New Kind of Life

Having Christ for our life also means that we will no longer "go it alone." His life in us does not prefer to live in solitude. His kind of life seeks out community. Notice how Jesus made a point of surrounding himself with companions. Even when his darkest hour found these friends sleeping through his pain, he still wanted them there. His life feels at home among others. In a way, it is only his life that truly can.

The fleshly race of the first Adam insulates itself from the vulnerability of true community. But the life of Jesus dives headlong into it, like a Vine that flourishes in its favorite soil. As this gospel frees us from the consuming egocentrism of the self life, we will find our world expanding to include those around us in a way that we have never experienced before. Rather than sending us off to work through these deeper aspects of the gospel in solitude, *God intends for his indwelling Spirit to produce a community of people who share his life together.*

Everything you have read up until this point may have spoken to you as an individual, and here many will set up camp and live. But God desires his people to learn to walk in the Spirit with the help of the larger Body of Christ. Remember how we saw earlier that the gospel doesn't stop after we get forgiven for our sins? We saw that the good news went on to deliver us from our very own selves. Well, that's not the end of the gospel, either. If you keep reading Romans through the twelfth chapter you will see that those who walk by the Spirit find themselves walking inevitably *toward the fellowship of the saints*. Paul's gospel to the Romans carries us forward into the practical expression of the Body of Christ because that is where the good news begins to bear its fruit. Let us turn now to see what else this gospel has in store.

Chapter Three:

Alone No More

We Americans are nothing if we are not individualists. We like doing things *our* way. We celebrate heroes like John Wayne and the Lone Ranger. In fact, many other countries think of the cowboy when they think of America. That wandering tough-guy of the Old West personifies the kind of rugged individualism that defines our culture. It should come as no surprise that our kind of Christianity leans heavily in that direction as well.

The ways of fallen humanity are quite familiar to us by now, aren't they? All things serve the unholy trinity of me, myself, and I. Self-interest becomes the basic motivation and preoccupation of every human being on the planet—including you and me. That is who we are "in ourselves." Ironically, this self-centered individualism eventually produces people compelled to conform to those around them. Human beings were not designed to be islands unto themselves. Ultimately, this inward turning upon the self produces a hollow center, a vacuum of identity and meaning, which the desperate creature then struggles to fill with anything and everything available.

As the years have rolled on, we fallen people have become experts in imitating one another. While declaring our independence from one another, we simultaneously mimic each other in everything from our clothing and our possessions to our language, our political views, and even our personalities.[1] American culture may very well be the most advanced manifestation of this malady to date. First we "cocoon" ourselves in our private suburban dwellings, cut off from the living, breathing human beings next door. Then we slavishly study and emulate the styles and philosophies of the familiar celebrities who enter our living rooms through our TV screens and our computers each night. From them we learn how to dress, what to eat, what to believe, and (God help us) how to treat members of the opposite sex. With careers that place hundreds of miles between us and our families of origin, we lose that sense of who we are until we are all too eager to be told what to think and how to live. It is no coincidence that America's primary export is entertainment. We have only one thing to sell that the rest of the world will buy: our culture.

Naturally, our more successful churches embody similar traits. With a weak gospel leaving us devoid of purpose, we

---

[1] For an insightful discussion of this paradox, see Gene E. Veith, *Postmodern Times* (Wheaton: Crossway Books, 1994), p.80ff.

look around at each other to find out what we should be doing. We become predictable in our conformity. The moment that someone "a little different" sets foot in our meetings, this becomes painfully clear. If he or she doesn't learn quickly how to talk, dress, and pray like the rest of us then his or her stay with us will not be long. Like our surrounding culture, we also demand that our churches meet our own psychological needs. We must have our twelve-step programs and our self-help books because that's ultimately what we're after. We'll flock to our bookstores and buy whatever new and shiny thing will make us look and feel like we're doing well in God's eyes.

Consumer Christianity

Consider how the typical evangelical Christian approaches the things of God. We initially receive the gospel because those who present it to us frame it in terms that are centered on us. They tell us: "Give your heart to Jesus and you'll be saved from hell," or "Receive Jesus into your heart so that your messed up life will take a turn for the better." Maybe they ask us: "Wouldn't you like to be with all the people you love in heaven when you die?" I'm not saying there aren't elements of these things inherent in the good news, because there are. But these are all about me, myself, and I. With a starting point like this, it is no wonder that we find it difficult to rise above self-interest in our Christian walk.

How about our approach to prayer? Prayer for most Christians is for two things: asking God to do things for you and asking God to do things for other people. Again, these aren't inappropriate things in themselves, but they take up far too much of our prayer life. Somewhere along the line we got a picture of God as a task-oriented Being who gave us prayer primarily as a way to make us as task-oriented as he is. But what would we be left with if we removed from our prayer lives all prayers that ask God to do something? We'd be left with simple communion. Sheer fellowship with our heavenly Father. Since when have you ever addressed your Father in prayer just to be with him, just to live in each other's company? What would our lives be like if that became the main purpose for seeking him in prayer? That's something to think about.

What about church? Why do people join a church? Why do they leave it? So many join a church because it offers them things that they want: a good children's program, professional music with talented musicians, a large single adult ministry, or maybe something even more specialized and more market-savvy like a support group for their specific needs (alcoholism, infertility, grief recovery, or weight loss). Churches that thrive numerically in this culture have either learned to offer a multitude of programs such as these or else they employ a talented and dynamic speaker to fill their pulpit. They have learned that these are the keys to drawing and keeping large crowds. When folks begin to leave a church, the most often heard phrase is "the pastor just wasn't feeding me." In the end it all comes down to this: Am I getting anything out of it?

Perhaps more problematic of all is how we approach and read the Bible itself. Since this book gives us our framework and our set of priorities for everything else we do, how we interpret it will set the course of our faith in its practical expression. So how do we read it? We come to it asking "What does it say to me?" We come to the Scriptures, perhaps by way of a daily devotional, hoping to get something we will need "to get us through the day." At first glance, this seems like a perfectly natural, pertinent question to ask; and perhaps ultimately that is where we will end up. But this approach fails to get beneath our individualistic, self-centered frame of reference. Since it cannot challenge that, we will not get far with this approach. We would do well to first ask, "To whom and for whom was this originally written?" While this may strike you as an academic starting point, I believe that finding the answer to that question may provide the needed backdrop against which God's mind and heart can become clear to us.

No Longer Alone

Let me illustrate. When I read that "we have the mind of Christ,"[2] I conclude that *I* have the mind of Christ and *I* set about trying to use it. Maybe I am trying to discern God's will in some matter; but no matter how long or how many times I come to him in prayer on the matter, I cannot seem to get to a place of peace about it. Multiple options seem right to me, with none of them clearly announcing "this is the way to go." So what went wrong? I took it to the Lord in prayer. I asked him what I should do. I thought I was supposed to have the mind of Christ.

---

[2] 1 Cor.2:16

But go back and read that declaration again. It says *we* have the mind of Christ. Do you see what I missed there? I am not a *we*. I am a me. As an individual, I do not have the mind of Christ. Sure, I have a piece of that mind—his Spirit is in me and I have his life. But I just have one piece. I need the rest of the saints together to see his mind really work in my life. That verse wasn't originally addressed to me, an individual. It was addressed to a church.[3] It was given to a community of people who together will access the mind of Christ, for that is their birthright.

The same thing applies to all the other great verses that we read for our instruction in the faith. Paul tells the believers in Rome that "all who are being led by the Spirit of God are sons of God."[4] If I conclude from this that I will be led by his Spirit, I have only marginally grasped what this verse is saying. Yes, I have his Spirit, and yes, I am a son of God. But notice the plural terms in that verse and in the ones around it. It says that the sons of God are led by his Spirit. That guidance grows in force and clarity as it is lived out in and among the communion of the saints. The Lord Jesus is our Good Shepherd, and he faithfully guides his flock. As a member of that spiritual community, I will experience his guidance. But I will meet with only frustration as I try to discern this leadership on my own, apart from my brothers and sisters.

I think this is a blind spot for those who have been turned on to the "deeper Christian life" through exceptional

---

[3] Many thanks to Gene Edwards for bringing this point home to me.
[4] Rom. 8:14

writers like Watchman Nee, Hudson Taylor, Ian Thomas, Norman Grubb, or even the mystics like Francois Fenelon and Madame Guyon. Writers such as these rediscovered and elucidated the forgotten dimensions of our gospel—our union with Christ, our identification with him in his death, resurrection, and ascension, and his life in us through his indwelling Spirit. But those who pick up these writings rarely go beyond the individual level in their application of these great truths. While much has been written about our "exchanged life" in Christ, few seem to realize that this exchange is meant to be lived out in community. Perhaps the churches they have known only disappointed them. Now they resign themselves to go it alone or with two or three other close friends. But we must not give up on the Church.

A Magnificent Obsession

Paul explained that he was driven by a mystery. He labored in the face of beatings and persecution because God had entrusted him with the stewardship of this mystery, which had been hidden for centuries but had now been made known. What is that mystery? It is "Christ in you, the hope of glory."[5] Only that translation doesn't quite get it. The Greek word for "you" in that verse is plural. Unfortunately, the English language does not have a word for that. In our language, "you" can mean one person or it can mean many. We need a word that means "you" in the plural. In the southeastern United States,

---

[5] Col.1:27

we have our own word for this: *y'all*. While our English teachers still insist that this little innovation is not appropriate, I think this gives us a better rendering of this significant statement. What is this mystery? It is *"Christ in y'all, the hope of glory."*

The indwelling of Christ, which realizes the kingdom of God, is a "corporate" indwelling — a communal event. Paul says to the Galatians that he was laboring among them "until Christ is formed in you." Once again, that "you" is plural. So a better translation would be "until Christ is formed among y'all." *Spiritual formation is a collective endeavor.* It's not about you, the individual, becoming more like Jesus. It's about him coming to reside among the saints in their relationships with each other. Whether the saints are gathered as a whole people or simply fellowshipping with one another in smaller pairs or groups, the incarnation continues. Christ's presence among his people grows more and more palpable as they come to realize their oneness with him. He comes to progressively "dwell in [our] hearts through faith" so that *"together with all the saints* [we] may be able to comprehend the breadth, length, height, and depth of the Love of Christ"* until the fullness of God is attained among his people.[6] All of this happens, not in the solitude of an individual Christian life, but in the community of the believers.

---

[6] Eph. 3:17-19

Paul's Introduction to the Church

Paul was fortunate enough to learn this lesson from the very beginning. The risen Christ spoke to Paul at his conversion, saying "Saul, Saul, why are you persecuting me?" He learned from the start that mistreating a follower of Jesus equals mistreating the Messiah himself. He is not separate from his people.

Luke reports that Paul spent his first few days as a believer meeting with the saints in Damascus,[7] learning their gospel and their way of life. I am certain that as he broke bread with them and listened to their stories, the news that Jesus had delivered to him on the way there was still echoing in his ears. As they shared a loaf of bread and a cup of wine, someone surely repeated Jesus' words: "This is my Body, which is for you." Perhaps it was then that he realized that Jesus wasn't talking about bread. As he looked around the room, it dawned on him that *these believers are his Body.* This meal gathers them together and celebrates that together they are the Body of Christ!

Years later, when the church in Corinth began to split into various factions and subgroups, Paul would remind them of the significance of this meal. "Since there is one bread, we who are many are one Body; for we all partake of the one bread."[8] Forgetting their union in Christ with one another, they had come to eat this meal in the same disjointed manner in which they lived and met.

---

[7] Acts 9:19
[8] 1 Cor.10:17

> Therefore when you meet together, it is not to eat the
> Lord's Supper, for in your eating each one takes his
> own supper first; and one is hungry and another is
> drunk. What!?... Do you despise the Church of God
> and shame those who have nothing?[9]

Economic, ethnic, and social distinctions had fractured the
church in Corinth. The meal itself had come to reflect their lack
of awareness that they are members of Christ's Body and
therefore members of one another as well. In so doing, they did
not "judge the Body rightly."[10] Paul's letter to them was
ultimately for this primary purpose: To remind them that they
are one with Christ and therefore one with each other.

"For even as the body is one and yet has many members,
and all the members of the body, though they are many, are one
body, so also is Christ."[11] This ranks among Paul's most earth-
shattering declarations. He does not say "just as the body has
many members, so also is *the church*;" he says "so also *is Christ*."
He makes no distinction here between Christ and the church.
As he began his letter to address the church's fragmentation, he
asked, "Can Christ be divided?"[12] The implied answer is "of
course not!" Yet dividing the church into rivaling factions
would do precisely that. It would be dividing Christ. This
cannot be. So he wrote to them to take them deeper into an
awareness of this great truth: We are the Body of Christ himself.
This is amazing news indeed.

---

[9] 1 Cor.11:20-22
[10] 1 Cor.11:29
[11] 1 Cor.12:12
[12] 1 Cor.1:13

One with Him Together

When I walk into a room, no one says "Oh, look, there's Neil's body." They say "There's Neil." The first concept is included in the second. If you hit me in the arm, I will not say "Why did you hit my body?" I will more likely ask "Why did you hit *me*?" That's because my arm is no less a part of me than is my head. It's all me. The same thing applies to the branches on a vine. When you look at a vine, you do not see two things—a vine in one place and branches in another. Instead, you see one vine, which includes the branches themselves. They are not separate things. The vine is both the trunk and the branches. So when Jesus said "I am the vine and you are the branches," He was telling us that we are no longer separate beings. We are now "in him"—each and every one of us who are called by his name.

Now we see what Jesus meant when he said "When you did it to the least of these brothers and sisters of mine, you did it to me."[13] People often quote this verse to encourage us to feed and clothe and care for everyone in need, regardless of who they are. Indeed, there are other verses that encourage us to do good to all people.[14] But this statement by Jesus focuses on "these brothers and sisters of mine." To make this beautiful declaration apply to all people robs it of its meaning. Those whom the Spirit of the Son has indwelt are united with him, so that caring for their needs is caring for him. Because we are one with him,

---

[13] Matt. 25:40 (TNIV)
[14] E.g., Gal.6:10; 1 Thess.5:15; Matt.5:45

when we touch a brother or sister in Christ we are touching Christ himself.

John makes it clear that loving God and loving his people are inseparable. "Whoever loves the Father loves the child born of him."[15] All those minute requirements we find in the Law of Moses ultimately boil down to this two-fold injuction: Love God and love each other. John makes it clear that these two imperatives interlock so completely that they really mean one thing. It means that we share the life of Christ with one another, as one organism. According to Jesus, our caring for one another is the distinguishing mark for his followers: "By this everyone will know that you are my disciples, if you have love for one another."[16]

Back to the Future

I imagine Paul would become physically sick watching the way we "celebrate" the Lord's Supper in our churches today. For starters, it has ceased to be a celebration at all. The way most churches observe this tradition looks more like a funeral than a celebration. Perhaps we get hung up on the part about "proclaiming his death" until his return.[17] This is understandable, since our gospel is stuck on payment for our sins.

When we read Paul's words about examining ourselves to see if we are drinking the cup and eating the bread "in an

---

[15] 1 Jn.5:1
[16] John 13:35 (NRSV)
[17] 1 Cor.11:26

unworthy manner," we conclude that this means we should be sure to feel really, really sorry about the death of Jesus on our behalf. We decide that all that suffering and pain on the cross is supposed to motivate us to do better from now on. Truly guilt is a powerful motivator. But this misses Paul's meaning completely! The unworthy manner of which he spoke referred to the Corinthian church fragmenting their fellowships according to class, race, and economic standing. Failing to discern the Body rightly means *failing to recognize that the church around you is one single organism*. It means failing to live in the light of that spiritual oneness with him and with one another.

I am certain that Paul would blow a gasket in some of our churches once we bring out our trays of individual crackers and tiny individual cups of grape juice. These are a clear testimony to our entrenched individualism. We each have our own separate little cup, and our own individually baked cracker. Far from celebrating our organic unity with one another as members of one single body, our tradition clearly says that we do not live in true community. It clearly states that we have very little awareness, if any, of our solidarity with one another or with Christ.

Our modern evangelical version of the Lord's Supper screams volumes about how we see ourselves as virtually independent little units assembled together for a brief moment in a nice, pretty environment. Each cracker sits alone on the shiny tray, hardly even touching the others around it. Likewise, we sit in our pews in our nice, pretty clothes, not bothering one another with our own inner struggles or weaknesses as we worship. This does not picture the oneness of the Body of Christ. It pictures our culture, and I believe it must grieve the Spirit of God.

One more thing must be mentioned here before we move on. A cracker and a sip of grape juice is not the Lord's *Supper*. It doesn't even qualify as a *snack!* The symbolism of spiritual sustenance — feeding on the presence of the Lord Jesus with us through his Spirit — has disappeared completely. The early believers fed one another with a whole meal, of which the bread and wine were simply a part. They gathered together, as regularly as once each week, to share a meal in which they celebrated their partaking of the Lord Jesus through his body and his blood.[18] This meal symbolizes feeding on him.[19] Protestant churches make little place for this kind of imagery because they hear too much Catholicism in it. But I think that after 500 years of reacting, we should consider revisiting the meaning of the "love feast" of the early believers.

Paul reminds us about God's people after their escape from Egypt: "They all ate the same spiritual food and they all drank the same spiritual drink, for they were drinking from a spiritual rock which followed them; and the rock was Christ."[20] The food and drink which sustained them through their journey

---

[18] Robert Banks, *Paul's Idea of Community* (Peabody: Hendrickson, 1994), p.81.

[19] Scholars have often noted that John's Gospel is the only gospel that not does not explicitly describe the Last Supper; John seems to replace it by presenting Christ as the bread of heaven (John 6) and as true drink for our thirsty souls (John 7).

[20] 1 Cor.10:3-5

to the promised land foreshadows the provision of Christ as our supply on our journey into the kingdom of God. That is why we gather together to have a meal, or better still a feast. We are celebrating the bounty of supply that we have together in Christ and we are anticipating the joyous wedding supper of the Lamb.[21] This should be an exciting, enjoyable occasion—more like a party than a funeral. Good news calls for a party!

Forsake Not the Assembling

We have seen that being the Body of Christ means that together we are one with Christ and therefore one with each other. My individual union with him is insufficient to accomplish God's purpose in saving me. He has always courted a collective people—a "them" with whom he may do his bidding. By taking both you and me into himself, making us one with him, he has made us one with each other.

No longer can we see ourselves as separate entities. Together we are parts of the same Body. We need each other as the hand needs the foot, or the tongue needs the ear, or the eye needs the lungs.[22] You meet Christ in ways that I do not, and I might see him in places that you do not. I may be having a "dry" week, or month (or year!), but your week with the Lord may have been refreshing and fruitful. I need your portion of Christ and you need mine. God did not make us islands; he made us

---

[21] Rev.19:9, See also Steve Atkerson, *Ekklesia* (Atlanta: NTRF, 2003), p.27-28.

[22] See 1 Cor.12.

parts of one Body. Our life together should attest to this reality, and so should our meetings.

In other words, both the way we live together and the way we assemble ourselves really matter. Granted, our meetings are only one facet of who we are. We will miss the point entirely if we make *the way we meet* our central focus. "Being the church" is not about proper mechanics. But our meetings do express who we are and why we are here. If we live together and function as the Body of Christ, then our meetings will express that fact in plain view.

On the other hand, when we do not live in the light of our oneness with him and with each other, our meetings and traditions will express that as well. There should be endless variety to the way that we meet since there will always be more of God's Spirit to express no matter how long we've been at it. We need not attempt to limit his self-expression in the church by trying to trace out one "right way" to meet. Having said that, however, we can say that some ways of meeting show forth the life of his Body better than others. Let us turn now to consider how we meet.

Chapter Four:

The Gathering of the Saints

D eep in the woods of North Mississippi, surrounded by 50,000 acres of tall pine trees, sits a Christian summer camp called Lake Forest Ranch. This camp manages to find the coolest counselors and work staff you could ever know. Somehow I was fortunate enough to work there the summer that I turned 21. Summer after summer, energetic young college students who work there encounter a deeper gospel like the one we've begun to explore in this book. They give and receive this bigger gospel every day, and every day they come together for what many of us consider the highlight of each day: staff meeting.

Don't let the name fool you — staff meeting was the best part of the day. Our camp directors carved this precious time out of our hectic schedules, away from all the campers, to meet together and discuss what was going on in our cabins and in our lives. We opened up to one another. We laughed with each other (and at each other). We prayed for one another and cried with each other. At the end of the summer we felt like we were leaving our closest family. While many of us never fully realized it, our time at LFR gave us a real taste of the communion of the saints.

In that open and intimate environment, we got a glimpse of the presence of Christ in one another and we were hooked. We got to see the life of Christ lived out in community, even if only for a short while. At an LFR reunion one year, I heard a youth minister confess that, deep down, his time at camp forever ruined him toward just "playing church" on Sunday morning.

That wasn't just a mass of individual Christians assembled for worship in the same spot. It was a group of people learning to give expression to the other-loving Spirit of Christ within them without most of the accessories of the Christian religion. It was raw community, and it was his life finding a way to become visible in our midst. You won't easily forget something like that, and afterwards you'll probably never be satisfied with anything less.

The Best Kind of Meetings

People are surprised when they find that their favorite meetings are the ones that are not led by any individual. Every year, more and more individuals are seeking out those environments which provide the most freedom for them to contribute to the edification of the Body of Christ, and which allow for others to do the same. Research by the Barna group demonstrates that the percentage of active, committed believers seeking alternative forms of church in this country has more than quadrupled over the last ten to fifteen years.[1] They are looking for a place where they can truly function.

Almost everyone has experienced at least one of those meetings where God's presence permeated every word spoken and every song sung. I believe that God intends for this experience to become a normal way of life for the Church rather than a rare treat. I do not believe that he intended for us to sit passively, silently listening for two to three hours every week in church while handing over 99% of the functioning to a handful of clergy or staff members. Of all people, those of us who identify as Protestants should know better than to allow a special "reverend" class of people to do all the planning and leading for us. Have we forgotten that our traditions originated upon the foundation of "the priesthood of all believers"?

---

[1] You can read about their discoveries in Barna's book entitled *Revolution* (Carol Stream: Tyndale, 2005), or else you can read a more detailed explanation of the group's research on their website: www.barna.org.

But most church meetings would entirely collapse if one day the preacher, the music leader, and the other staff members all decided to stay home. A few key members of the Body have come to function for the whole. Our current situation looks like a dialogue I once read:

> "How are you doing?"
> "Pretty well, under the circumstances."
> "What are the circumstances?"
> "Well, I have a very effective arm. It moves with quite a bit of animation. But then I have my bad leg."
> "What's wrong with it?"
> "I guess it's paralyzed. At least it doesn't do much except twitch once a week or so, but that's nothing compared with the rest of me."
> "What's the problem?"
> "From all appearances, the rest is dead. At least it stinks and bits of flesh are always falling off. I keep it well covered. About all that's left beyond that is my mouth, which fortunately works just fine. How about you?"[2]

Tozer once said "the presence [of God] and the manifestation of the presence are not the same . . . He is manifested only when and as we are aware of his presence."[3] The same thing can be said about the Body of Christ. Walk into any gathering of Baptists, Methodists, Episcopalians, Catholics, Presbyterians, Assemblies of God, Community Churches, the Vineyard, etc., and you will surely find the members of the Body of Christ present, because believers are there. But the *presence* of

---

[2] Jim Elliff, http://www.ccwonline.org/sbc.html.
[3] Tozer, p.64.

the Body doesn't necessarily indicate the actual *functioning* of the Body. In fact, even in a full auditorium, only three or four individuals will run the entire meeting. This is like having one giant tongue standing up in front of a room full of ears. Imagine if only three or four parts of your physical body were actually functioning right now. A doctor would surely note the time and call the coroner.

Church staff members are always lamenting about how difficult it is to motivate church members to participate and share the burden for activities in the church. The irony is that they actively perpetuate the very predicament that so frustrates them. Pastors are burned out and members are bored. But when anyone snaps out of it and suggests a different way, he becomes perceived as a "loose cannon" and a liability to the congregation. (In case you're wondering, no, that wasn't my experience. I left before that could ever happen).

It's Alive!

Like a newborn baby or a freshly plowed field, the birth/planting of churches in the first century began with utter simplicity. Like any living thing, they had structure "wired into them" at their conception, although it took months or years to see that fully develop. Life develops organically. But we have become accustomed to thinking of the Body of Christ as an institution—a machine—rather than a living organism. Most churches today begin with preselected staff members, accompanied by 5-year plans for growth (often with a very expensive building program soon to follow). Like Dr.

Frankenstein, we seem to believe that if we assemble all the right parts of the body and supply a jolt of electricity, we can create a living thing. Instead we find ourselves fighting a monster. The Church is not a machine. A machine is an organization; the Church is a living organism.

Here's a test to determine whether our churches are living organisms or machines: Do they basically look and perform the same way week after week, year after year, and decade after decade? Life is full of variety and change, while machines repeat identical movements over and over again as long as you keep them running. For example, a 2006 model car will still be a 2006 model car fifty years later. Parts will need replacing, but only by identical parts. On the other hand, a 2006 model human being will look quite different fifty years later. In fact, biologists tell us that every cell in the body will be new within seven years.

Life requires a dynamic, living organism to contain it. The rigid gears of a machine would only kill it. No sensible person would put leg braces on a perfectly healthy baby just to ensure that she grow legs of the right length and proportion. Yet that is how we approach spiritual things. We typically begin by declaring that a healthy church should have this and do that, and therefore we should "facilitate" those things right from the start. "You do not have in mind the things of God, but the things of man."[4]

---

[4] Matt.16:23

Jesus confronted the Pharisees one day because they, too, misunderstood the dynamic nature of the Spirit. They devoted great energy to upholding the traditions that had been handed down to them. Perhaps those traditions had once communicated life to those who created them, but now they were just getting in the way. Like old wineskins trying to contain new wine, their religious practices no longer matched the direction of God's activity.

At this point you might say, "Hey, I already belong to a church. Doesn't that mean that I'm already a part of his Body?" That may be true, in principle. But you're not really experiencing his Body when a group of people show up to watch a handful of clergy function in ways that should be the responsibility of everyone. Afterwards, everyone returns home (miles away) to a typically sequestered American lifestyle. It may very well be that we have some cultural and sociological hurdles to jump if we are ever to restore the New Testament concept of the Christian community. But before we consider what to do about that, let's look at a few basic things that we must realize.

Behold the Power of Tradition

First, I will assume that anyone with access to a New Testament knows that a church is not a building made out of brick and mortar (a thought totally foreign to the early believers). It has become tradition for us to look at a building and call that "a church." When we walk into that place, we have a long list of rules and expectations about how one is to behave "in God's house." You don't bring food or drink into the sanctuary (God forbid), you don't run in church, and for Pete's sake you don't talk during the service or you'll mess everything up! When we go to this place, we dress differently, we talk differently, and we even smile differently. Our activity in that place has become so different from the rest of our normal lives that it's no wonder so many find it irrelevant.

We should know better than this. Our God does not dwell in buildings made by human hands.[5] We should not walk into an auditorium with pews and high-vaulted ceilings and call that "God's house." The Church is God's people, who themselves make up his dwelling place on the earth. *We* are God's house. We are the Temple of the living God. For starters, we are going to have to start making that more explicit in our thoughts and our speech with one another.

Second, I must restate that, if your concept of a thriving church involves less than 5% of those present doing the leading (teaching, planning, praying, song-selecting, etc.), then you are letting centuries of tradition guide your thinking more than the story of the New Testament Church. Go back and re-read the story of the early Church. Put the letters to the churches back in order so that they fit within the story. If you do that you will learn that so many of our traditions do not find biblical support.

For example, some will point to the church in Jerusalem in the book of Acts to prove that someone should always be "up front" preaching and leading. But as you follow the story beyond

---

[5] Acts 7:48

the initial birthing of the church in Jerusalem (even more so in the other cities), you will see that the "up front" leaders fade to the background and "the brothers and sisters" take over. That kind of "front and center" ministry serves to establish the Christian community at the beginning. However, if it continues to dominate the gathering of the saints, over time it will stifle the functioning of the other members of the Body.

A third thing we must gather the nerve to confront is our practice of the pastoral office itself. So many people assume that, since this tradition has been established for hundreds of years, it must be God's will for the Church. But imagine how that kind of thinking would have altered the outcome of the Reformation. What if Martin Luther had concluded along with everyone else that, since paying indulgences for salvation from purgatory was widely practiced, it must be the way things should be? Where would we be today if he had never faced this question squarely? Every once-in-a-while folks have to ask hard questions. We must be willing to let go of those things which are not consistent with God's revealed intent for the Church.

The present day function of the pastor-as-CEO comes more from tradition than it does from the New Testament story.[6] He does not dominate the life of the early Church the way he does in our day. In fact, the word "pastor" only appears once in a list of other gifts, alongside a number of functions that many churches today would swear no longer exist. Does your church

---

[6] Frank Viola and George Barna have compiled an entire book about how we developed our most dogmatic church traditions. The book is entitled *Pagan Christianity* (Carol Stream: Tyndale, 2008).

have an apostle? Or a prophet? Or an evangelist? Many will answer "No," although they may add that they have a minister of music, or of youth, or of finance. I am personally unconvinced that the Body of Christ should even be broken up according to the kinds of demographic categories to which we have accommodated our ministries.

As for the pastor himself, his function *as we maintain it today* cannot be found in the story of the earliest believers. You will not find an account of the meeting of the first century Church in which a guy gets up in front and preaches every week for half an hour or more. Yet this is the center of our Protestant church tradition. If you remove the Sunday morning sermon, you remove the centerpiece of the worship service itself.

So let's look at the evangelical worship service, then. Is that based in Scripture? When pressed, most would admit that it's not necessarily an issue of biblical support. It is more of a tradition that we've developed over the years, and they like it that way, thank you very much! We start with an organ prelude and a call to worship, which is sung by a specially trained choir. After an official greeting by someone on staff, we sing a few preselected hymns (who got to pick them?) and listen to some "special music" sung by either the choir or by a vocally gifted soloist. Then we sit very still and very quiet for a long time while the pastor delivers his sermon. Some very official-looking men will collect our tithes and offerings either just before or just after the sermon. The sermon will always conclude with an invitation—even if the sermon itself contained nothing that would prompt it. Finally there will be another song sung to dismiss the audience, who sat so passively throughout the entire performance that their presence was scarcely required for the service to even happen!   At some time during this ritual the audience may be instructed to stand and shake the hands of three or four people around them.   This they call "a time of fellowship."   Was *this* what God had in mind when he encouraged us not to forsake the assembling of ourselves together?

A Peek into the First Century

One of the fascinating facts about the New Testament is that it says almost nothing about how to meet. Both the gospels and the letters are strangely silent on the matter. Ultimately that is a good thing. How boring would our faith be if we had only one way to meet?   Even if we could discern *the way* the first-century believers met, we would not want to copy them like religious robots. We don't live in the first century. We do not occupy the same time or space that they did. But that does not separate us from them as much as we may think. We still share a common spiritual life with them.   Because of this, it would be profitable for us to ask how the life of Christ showed up in the gatherings of our first-century brothers and sisters.

The only place that actually lets us peek into a weekly Christian meeting in the first century is 1 Corinthians 14:26-31:

> When you assemble, each one has a psalm, has a teaching, has a revelation, has a tongue, has an interpretation. Let all things be done for edification. If anyone speaks in a tongue, it should be by two or at the most three, and each in turn, and one must

interpret; but if there is no interpreter, he must keep
silent in the church; and let him speak to himself and
to God. Let two or three prophets speak, and let the
others pass judgment. But if a revelation is made to
another who is seated, the first one must keep silent.
For you can all prophesy one by one, so that all may
learn and all may be exhorted.

For starters, try finding a leader in that meeting. Who is in
charge? The Holy Spirit is the only real leader in such an unled,
unfacilitated meeting. There are other things we can learn from
this little snapshot of the church in Corinth, but this single detail
is significant by itself.

Next Sunday morning, when your minister stands to
deliver his message, I dare you to do what this passage instructs.
Whenever God illumines or reveals something to you that may
be of benefit to the congregation, stand up and share it with the
whole church. What do you think will happen? They will surely
usher you out the door. I realize that for some this only
illustrates how verses of scripture should not be divorced from
their context or intended audience. But the absurdity of my
suggestion should move us to ask why our way of meeting is so
fundamentally different from theirs.

Most people today naturally assume that the minister has
more scriptural justification to speak than anyone else there. But
one man cannot adequately speak for God on his own, every
week of every year, for twenty years! God has much more to say
to his people than can be spoken through one or two people. It
is no wonder that so many people hop from church to church,

saying that "the pastor just wasn't feeding me." He was never meant to.

The Way We Meet Matters

When we gather we are reassembling Christ himself in visible, audible, touchable form. Our meetings should attest to that fact. Remember that we are him, reassembled. That's what being his Body means. Until all of him is free to function, he will not be fully seen. Some rationalize our present practices, saying that our diverse gifts are exercised somewhere outside of the meeting. To some degree that is true. But our meetings demonstrate who we are. When we gather all in one place, Christ must be seen in all his fullness. He should not be hidden underneath our centuries of ritual and tradition. Put differently, our meetings must not look like anything else in this world—certainly not a meeting of a business, a university, or any other man-made institution. Jesus said that we are not of this world any more than he is of this world.[7] So why do our assemblies look like a concert, or a shareholders' meeting for a corporation, with a CEO, a board of directors, and then "the little people" watching quietly?

Christ is in you, wanting to speak. Christ is in another, wanting to sing. Through another he wishes to show care. Through another he wants to challenge and exhort. Another member of his Body can hardly contain her desire to praise him for something. Every part of him is bursting at the seams to be displayed. If we believe he is alive and in us, then the way we

[7] John 17:14, 16

meet should provide opportunity for this expression to take place. Let us begin with an overwhelming awareness of the presence of Christ among us, filling and guiding the members of his Body.

Next we should take back the meetings that are rightfully ours. Only Christ is head of his Body, and no one but he should take center stage when we gather. We need only to raise our expectation for the Lord Jesus to speak through his whole Body, not merely through one or two people. It may be true that some in each fellowship will be gifted to teach more than others, but this does not mean they have to dominate the meeting. We must be willing to give the rest of the Body a chance to prove that "every joint can supply" the needs of the church. We must even be willing to risk failure in the process. How else can we move forward?

Perhaps we can start by admitting that our predicament arose from fallen humanity's natural tendency to appoint kings to lead us. We naturally look for a CEO to guide us. But I'm convinced that any fresh movement of God's Spirit will radically challenge our positions of leadership, our multi-million dollar building budgets, and our programs of perpetual motion. God will not pour his new wine into an old wineskin. We will need a new wineskin—a totally new way to meet.

A New Way to Live

Of course, our meetings are just the tip of the iceberg. The deeper issue involved here is that the gospel calls us into becoming a true community. The kingdom of God is not a once a week thing. It happens every day. We live it and breathe it. The way we structure our whole lives speaks to the nature of this kingdom. Paul encourages the Church to live out every aspect of daily life "doing all in the name of the Lord Jesus."[8]

This means that we must ask some hard questions about how to be followers of Jesus in the midst of our own culture. Can we position ourselves geographically so that we can be more involved in one another's lives? Must we live so far away from those with whom we meet? Can we position the church so that interaction with the world around us can happen in a relational, organic way? We must be willing to take some practical steps to see just how much this gospel can do. Would you be willing to relocate in order to be closer together with other believers? Would you allow the kingdom of God to infringe upon your American dream?

I am often amazed at how many intelligent people stumble upon the deeper things of the Lord only to remain exactly as they were before. Somehow they decide that these glorious things should be tucked away in their own hearts without disturbing the status quo. In the end they change nothing, and the religious machinery just keeps chugging along. This is where the rubber really meets the road. When you set your mind on altering our traditions, you will find yourself up against these very practical things. It may be that most will find that they simply can't leave it all behind. For those ready to try

---

[8] Col.3:17

something new, however, I will later suggest a few things that can be done.

A Growing (Yet Dying) Trend

There is in fact a global movement happening which is bringing back a more simplistic and intimate form of worship. People all over the world are discovering that small groups are where it's at. On the international mission field, evangelicals have long known that small home groups work best. They require no overhead costs. They are mobile. They provide the relational environment that long-term international evangelism demands. Most importantly to them, home groups can multiply more rapidly than congregational churches because of their distributed leadership model and their natural potential for personal impact.

Here in the United States as well, we are seeing a surge of interest in smaller, more interactive forms of worship. Traditional congregational worship often does not appeal to the "unchurched," who grew up without much exposure to that peculiar vocabulary and style of music. Many without an evangelical upbringing will have little use for the impersonal formalities that come with that kind of scene. The ideological confidence of its leaders may even strike them as unwarranted arrogance. In other words, traditional churches are just too incongruous with the rest of our culture to lure them in. They feel more at home in a small, intimate group of believers who gather to encourage one another and worship in a more personal, interactive and participatory manner.

But what about people who are already believers? I mentioned earlier how Barna has found that large numbers of evangelicals are themselves leaving traditional church for other alternatives. Once Christians get a taste of authentic, open interaction with one another they learn to make room for this beautiful thing, even if it means getting rid of the traditions that have demanded their allegiance in the past.

In general, the house church/simple church model is catching on in cities across the United States. A house church movement began in the late 1990s and has slowly built up momentum since then. Sometimes these churches start out as an offshoot of a larger congregational church. Other times they begin from scratch with two or three families seeking something new. Lately they are more likely to start in coffeehouses and in college towns. They start out in so many unique ways that you can hardly describe how it happens. But the one thing that most of them have in common is that *they will not last for more than three or four years.*[9] While they start with enthusiasm and expectation, they mostly fizzle and break up after a short while. Why is that?

Didn't See That Coming

I'm sure someone could make a living by analyzing these dissipations and diagnosing them. But I've got a strong notion

---

[9] To see what I mean, you could periodically check house church databases like the ones on Sites Unseen (www.zoecarnate.com) and on House Church Central (www.hccentral.com).

that the real reasons will escape the notice of the statistician. Of course, a few of the reasons are easier to spot. Most groups are started by people with a need for control. They find it difficult to relinquish leadership when the time comes. In the end many groups will wind up copying what they did before, only now they do it in more comfortable clothes.

Groups which press on into true community will find an unexpected byproduct of the fellowship of the Body of Christ. They get their expectations built up so easily by dreams and theories about what the church should be and how it should work. What they probably didn't count on was *the sufferings of Christ becoming theirs as a community.* Once this unwelcome intrusion creeps up in the meetings of an unprepared group of Christians, people sometimes leave skidmarks on their way out the door.

It never occurs to most of us that sharing in the life of Christ involves sharing in his sufferings, too. The moment the heat gets turned up on a fledgling house church, folks start dropping like flies and giving up altogether. But this need not be. A church that understands what it is getting into can be better prepared to deal with the crises when they come—and they most certainly will come as long as human beings are involved. It doesn't matter if they're saved or unsaved, carnal, backslidden, or super-spiritual. They all have a fallen nature that will complicate the beautiful dreams of the Church in all of our minds. But the church that ventures out into this territory with its eyes open just might learn to deal with that calling.

Above all else, they must come to see that in fact this *is* our calling. We share in the life of Christ together, even unto the sharing of his dying. In the next two chapters, we will look at what this calling entails.

Chapter Five:
The Dark Side of the Gospel

Americans do not like to suffer. In fact, nothing could be more contrary to a nation founded on the principles of life, liberty, and the pursuit of happiness. Modern comforts have accustomed us to expect quick and easy solutions for all of life's difficulties. Whenever we are in pain, we swallow pain relievers. When we are sick, we take antibiotics. When we are hungry, we have thousands of food choices available through our well-stocked, well-lit supermarkets and our fast food restaurants. If we don't feel like driving in our comfortable cars to get these things, we can have it all delivered to our doors with a phone call or a click of a mouse. In the same way, with the click of a button, we can choose from hundreds of brands of clothing for any style and any season. If we can't afford the expense of the things that we want, we simply call on the gods of American culture: Visa, MasterCard, and American Express. We will do anything except deny ourselves the things that we want.

For this reason, I remain doubtful that Christ-filled expressions of the Church will ever be in great supply in this country. It saddens me to say that, because I want to see what the shared life of Christ looks like in my own country. But attempts to bring this life on American soil have routinely met with failure. Groups seeking to experience this life together seldom remain intact for more than a few years, or else they lose their vitality by gradually reverting back to the religious patterns they once rejected. I believe the reason for this can be found in the striking incompatibility of the character of God in Christ with the self-loving, self-serving culture of modern (and post-modern) America. We simply don't know how to lose, and that separates us from the deeper things of God.

Getting to Know the Other Side of God

Whatever is true of Christ, the head, will be true also for his Body. If he is righteous, loving, and gracious, then his Body will likewise be righteous, loving, and gracious. If he is victorious over sin, Satan, the self-life, and even sickness and death, then his Body will also experience his surpassing power over each of these things. But he is also a man of sorrows, acquainted with grief, and *it is his nature to lose for the sake of those whom he loves*. For this reason, as we come to know the life of

Christ lived out in community, we will move into a fuller experience of his dying for others as well.

If God is love, and love means giving your self for the sake of another, then loss must be foundational to the character of God. Horace Bushnell once wrote that "There is a Gethsemane hid in all love."[1] Indeed we see something fundamental to God's nature when we see his sufferings for his people. For centuries, theologians have debated the meaning of Revelation 13:8 where we learn that Christ was "slain from the foundation of the world." They puzzle and quibble over a theological chicken-or-egg question which asks: "Did God's plan of salvation *result* from the fall of Man or did it somehow *cause* it in the first place?" Whatever the right answer, of this we can be certain: We would never have known God's love for sinners if sin had never entered the world. With the fall of mankind, however, the forgiving, self-sacrificing grace of God became evident to all. I believe his loving, losing nature could become apparent only within a context of a creation in rebellion. And since his character shows up most clearly in a crucifixion, somehow that undergirds everything else that has happened.

Consider how from the beginning God decreed that most living things would multiply and reproduce: by *seeds*. This ubiquitous little invention of God predates the fall of mankind, yet it speaks of dying in order to produce new life.[2] As Jesus

---

[1] Horace Bushnell, *The Vicarious Sacrifice* (New York: Scribner, 1891), p.47. Also he says, "Love is a principle essentially vicarious in its own nature, identifying the subject with others, so as to suffer their adversities and pains, and taking on itself the burden of their evils" (p.42).

[2] Once again I am indebted to Gene Edwards for pointing this out.

said, "Unless a grain of wheat falls into the ground and dies, it remains alone; but if it dies it bears much fruit."[3] Now we know that creation pictures God's character for us.[4] Any great work of art expresses something of the artist who created it. The cosmos is no different. Everywhere we look we see little object lessons which speak to us about the God who made it all. So what do we learn from a seed? We learn that life reproduces itself by giving itself up and dying in order to increase and multiply.

For another illustration of his character, consider the roles which God gave us as beings created in his image. Like the seeds, we also multiply and produce offspring; only we soon discover that raising children really "takes it out of you." From the moment they are born until the moment you die, these beautiful gifts of God will cause you to lose your self in pieces every day and in every way imaginable. Parenting requires a daily (no, an hourly) death to self-interest, driving many to abandon the whole thing. But this role that we play brings us into a picture of his grace toward us. In some small way we get to experience a little of what God experiences as a loving, self-sacrificing Father.

Marriage works the same way, doesn't it? Marriage requires a constant giving over of ourselves for the sake of another, so that we cannot often do the things that we like. The needs of "that other person" daily demand that you sacrifice

---

[3] John 12:24
[4] Rom.1:19-20

your will for the good of another. Once again we find ourselves living out an object lesson of God's grace toward us.

Hosea learned to identify with his Creator in a special way when God told him to marry a promiscuous woman. God presented Hosea with a unique opportunity to walk "in his steps," learning to love and give himself over for the good of a woman who would not always love him back. Hosea repeatedly endured the rejection of her infidelity only to seek her reconciliation to himself. In this he was learning to identify with the emotional life of God. Through those terrible years Hosea learned to know his God like few ever had before.

Now God has called his many new sons and daughters to step up into our own kind of identification with him, so that we may know him better, too.[5] As we come to experience the life of Christ among his people, we should expect to see both his dying and his rising again in our daily lives. "To you it has been granted for Christ's sake, not only to believe in him, but also to suffer for his sake."[6] Peter affirmed the same thing: "You have been called for this purpose, since Christ also suffered for you, leaving you an example for you to follow in his steps."[7]

At the turn of the 20th century, Charles Sheldon popularized that last phrase with his novel *In His Steps*.[8] In this book, Sheldon tells the story of a group of people who decide to pattern their lives around answering the question "What would

---

[5] Phil.3:10-11

[6] Phil.1:29

[7] 1 Pet.2:21

[8] Charles Sheldon, *In His Steps* (Grand Rapids: Baker, 1984).

Jesus do?" This simple question propels them into a new kind of life, and readers have drawn inspiration from their adventures ever since. But this idea can easily lend itself to that overly religious "imitation of Christ" that I mentioned in Chapter Two. We can tap into the wellspring of his nature because he is in us, not because we are merely trying to act like he would act.

If we will look more closely at the context of Peter's statement about walking in his steps, we see that it indicates something far more specific. Walking in his steps means enduring hardship and suffering for his sake. Sometimes it comes from godless rulers, ruthless employers, or uncaring family. Whatever their source, hardship and mistreatment give us an opportunity to unite ourselves in spirit with the Lord Jesus because those moments bring out his character most clearly. His patient endurance and his deep trust in his Father's justice can be ours when those moments come. In suffering we identify with this Man of Sorrows, and we unite our hearts to his in the process. Just as it was his nature to grow through suffering,[9] so it is the Church's nature to grow through suffering as well.

Daily Crosses

Where does this suffering come from? Any place and every place! I should first clarify that every bad thing that happens to you isn't necessarily a cross. "Stuff happens," as they say, and it happens to everybody without exception.

---

[9] Heb.2:10

People who do not know the Lord experience pain, loss, death, and loneliness, too. But these are not crosses. They are just the symptoms of a broken world doing what it ordinarily does.

Sometimes the difficulties you face in life stem from mistakes that you've made—poor judgment calls on your part. We reap what we sow, and we must take responsibility for the choices that we make and the habits that we form. We learn nothing from our mistakes if we label every unpleasant consequence "a cross." For example, don't pursue a romantic relationship with an emotionally abusive person only to blame it on "providence" once he or she turns on you. Let's be reasonable about this.

The other side to this matter is that, paradoxically, God *does* have his hand in the things that happen to you. He can and does take the choices you make, turning them into useful things. "He disciplines those whom he loves."[10] In other words, bad things happen to everybody—good people and "bad" people. But our Father in heaven will use the pain and loss that afflict his children for constructive ends. Joe Schmoe may lose his job and turn bitter and untrusting. You, on the other hand, may experience the same thing and find it turned into gold. Your losses can make room for Christ's presence to increase in your heart so that nothing is truly lost in the end.

Christians may get at least one thing that unbelievers do not experience: Persecution for the name of Jesus.

> If you were of the world, the world would love its own; but because you are not of the world... the world

[10] Heb.12:6

> hates you. Remember the word that I said to you, 'A
> slave is not greater than his master.' If they persecuted
> me, they will also persecute you.[11]

Blatant persecution for the name of Christ continues to this day in countries like China, Saudi Arabia, and Sudan, while Christians in the United States enjoy social respectability and freedom of religion. I suppose it is no coincidence that both persecution *and spiritual vitality* are missing from our American churches today. They seem to go hand in hand. When the community of the saints ceases to look or behave any differently from the rest of the world, there is little reason for them to be hated by it. Ironically, the religious freedom which enables churches and ministers to operate in broad daylight has erased almost all traces of that external pressure which would otherwise drive the Church to a desperate dependence upon the Spirit. Because of this, we miss a powerful opportunity for knowing and identifying with the Man of Sorrows.

Raw Community

But suffering in the Body of Christ has more than just external sources. When people decide as a group to share their lives together in an intimate way, it does not take long to discover the other great source of suffering which God has provided: *our brothers and sisters in Christ.* While institutional church traditions pad and protect individuals from one another, true community exposes us for who we really are. We are fallen

---

[11] John 15:19-20

human beings for whom self-preservation and self-promotion have become a deeply-rooted way of life. Our quirks and tricks hide well behind the antiseptic veneer of evangelical Sunday morning worship. But underneath those pressed suits, that flawless make-up, and those conditioned smiles lurks a whole complex of warped thoughts and habits which go untouched by the usual religious activity. If you remove the padding of evangelical church tradition and place a group of believers into a more intimate, communal experience of the church, they won't look so good anymore.

In the more authentic context of true Christian community, you will discover that nothing can cause more pain than a member of the Body of Christ. The things we are capable of in this environment! You wouldn't believe some of the stories we could tell. Your Christian walk transforms into something completely different while living in close quarters with other believers (whatever form that takes) without the larger personal space afforded by a pew, a sanctuary, and a Sunday School classroom. The weaknesses and burdens of your brothers and sisters cling to you as if they were your own, because now they might as well be. This is "life together," and it ain't your grandmother's kind of church! Stuff happens here that makes everything else look like a walk in the park.

Living like this, we become vulnerable to the personal problems that each person has shouldered alone until now. We bear one another's burdens.[12] In our church, we have only just

---

[12] Gal.6:2

begun to discover this aspect of "suffering one another." For example, when a sister in the church makes life difficult for everyone because of her quirks and neuroses, our first reaction is annoyance. We wish she would just get over herself and move on with life. Then we begin to realize that those things that are weighing her down may be burdens that she cannot cast off. She may be stuck with them for life. But now she does not have to shoulder them alone. Together we can come beside her and share the burden of her past, her memories, her genes, or even her addictions. We can lighten her load a little by spreading it around. Adding her troubles to our own lives may stretch us to our capacity, but something beautiful is happening there. The Body of Christ is doing what it does best. It is building itself up in love.[13]

Sometimes these trials come at us through the deliberate mistreatment of a brother or sister. Other times they are the unintentional fallout of a weary brother's psychosis being spread around for everyone to endure. Either way, these pressures have a way of sifting us out like wheat. They produce and reveal things in us that we never would have discovered any other way. And that is how it should be. Paul once said "these things must happen in order that those who are approved may be known."[14] While suffering and mistreatment are not the ultimate goal of the Christian community, they are an indispensable part of God's sovereign dealings with his people.

---

[13] Eph.4:16
[14] 1 Cor.11:19

A New Kind of Love

Most of us don't get to choose who will be a part of our community of faith. Jesus, on the other hand, *deliberately chose* his community and included Judas Iscariot from the beginning. "I chose you, yet one of you is a devil," he said.[15] In order to fulfill his role as Messiah, he needed a betrayer among his closest companions. With Judas present, Jesus' washing of their feet takes on a whole new meaning, doesn't it? After washing Judas' feet, he says "a new command I give you, that you love one another *even as I have loved you.*"[16] This indeed is a new kind of love – love in the face of utter betrayal.

This is the kind of love that he seeks to express in us today. You can be sure that he will require a backdrop of mistreatment to make his point. It is when Christian turns against Christian that God's covering, forgiving love stands out the most. When your brother or your sister turns against you and you do not repay evil for evil, in that moment you have demonstrated the life of Christ in you. Upon such moments the Church will step higher toward his purpose in calling them.

I cannot emphasize enough that this doesn't really happen in a Sunday-and-Wednesday-only kind of church. Apart from an intimate experience of Christian community, this kind of love and loss could hardly be possible. People have to be truly under your skin for them to hurt you. Sitting next to them for an hour or two as you both listen to a Sunday School lesson or a sermon will never provide the kind of context that I

---

[15] John 6:70
[16] John 13:34

am describing. A few minutes of conversation over doughnuts and coffee doesn't cut it, either. You have to really know each other for this to work.

As a teacher, I work alongside people who regularly deal with mistreatment and disrespect from kids less than half their age. Teaching high school in a lower-income area like mine brings a daily dose of cursing, criticism, and defiance from the very individuals we are trying the hardest to help. Some days it's too much for even the most professional educators to bear. Almost every week I see someone melt down because of the treatment he or she must take from the students—in addition to the pressure of the professional expectations put upon him or her.

But when I hold the abuse that I see in that environment up against the pain that can be inflicted upon a person within an intimate community of believers, there is no comparison. The church wins, hands down. No one at work can hurt me like someone at home can. And for me, I live amongst an extended family of a couple of dozen brothers and sisters who have the capacity to cut me to my core by virtue of who we are to one another. This kind of vulnerability comes with the territory of living in the Body of Christ.

So many writers and ministers who speak about the deeper Christian life champion a "victorious Christian life" message with no cross or suffering required. Few have ever touched this kind of under-your-skin community. That's why they so rarely speak of this kind of dying which comes from bearing with one another when we are at our worst. At best, the cross may surface with an academic tone about it. Their words often lack the ring of experiential knowledge.

This happens because the individual Christian life conceals the subtle religiosity of the flesh. Life alone may give you the illusion that you are further along than you really are. But once you step into an authentic expression of the Body of Christ, that mirage will evaporate in a matter of seconds. In that place, you will truly discover what it means to "trust him who judges righteously"[17] even in the face of your own little crucifixion. On the other hand, you will also learn what it means to be carried by your brothers and your sisters. In this intimate community you will find a "safe place" to unload your burdens, and to be seen for who you are–warts and all.

Under a Sovereign Hand

I suppose I should state clearly that all of this assumes the complete sovereignty of God in our daily lives. You cannot see the hand of God in the perverse actions of fallen people if you do not believe in his absolute control over the course of your life. Unfortunately, our post-enlightenment education has predisposed many of us against the idea of *providence*. Providence means that all things are seen as being from God's own hand. In case you never noticed, that belief undergirds all that the writers of scripture have to say to us (both New Testament and Old). Paul said that "God works all things

---

[17] 1 Pet.2:23

together for the good of those that love him."[18] Elsewhere he says that "God works all things according to the counsel of his will."[19]

We tend to view events in our lives as the result of "second causes," attributing them to things like nature, fallen humanity, or even chance. On the surface that may be true. The apostles and prophets, however, are unanimous in telling us that the sovereign working of God is underneath all of these things. Jesus himself put it this way: "Are not two sparrows sold for a penny, yet not one of them falls to the ground apart from your Father. Even the hairs on your head are numbered."[20] By that last statement he didn't mean that God merely *knows* how many hairs crown your head. The force of his language is stronger than that. He means to say that God has *determined* something even as insignificant as the amount of hair on your head (which to many men is not so insignificant!)

Some today would call this a *premodern* view of the world — too simplistic and naïve for well educated people like us to believe. Ancient peoples saw lightning and heard thunder and said, "Behold the work of God." Surely our more scientifically sophisticated understanding of the world rules out this kind of simplicity, right? I would argue that it's just as likely that our modern outlook on life comes from an overly simplistic view of time and space. Let me explain:

---

[18] Rom.8:28
[19] Eph.1:11
[20] Matt.10:29 (NIV)

As I look outside my window I see a tree. Did God make that tree? I believe he did. You may think I'm being foolish, because that tree is no older than a decade or two. You may argue that God's creation of the universe dates back either thousands or billions of years, depending on your view of creation. You may tell me that God created the first trees but that he did not in fact create *that* tree. A landscaper may have put it here or else nature randomly dropped a seed in that spot years ago. While this explanation seems to be more sophisticated than mine, I believe it is actually more simplistic. It fails to account for the fact that, from God's timeless perspective, the moment of creation and this very moment are not separate things at all. God did not simply create one moment long ago and sit back to watch the show (more on God's timelessness in Chapter Eight).

The drama you see unfolding around you is in fact a story being told by the most creative Storyteller ever known. Apparently random events present you with challenge after challenge until you are scarcely able to take another moment. These are not accidental; they come to you tailor-made from your sovereign Father in heaven. He works all things for the good of his children (assuming that you don't define "good" in terms of the absence of pain or difficulty!). David said it beautifully: "In your book were written all the days ordained for me before one of them came to be."[21] Like David, we must see that even the most minute details of our lives have been

---

[21] Psalm 139:16

choreographed by our Father for his purposes. The forces of nature and even the actions of other people follow his design.

When Jesus hung on the cross, he did not blame the people around him for his execution. He looked through these second causes and cried, "Father, why have *you* forsaken me?" In the end it was his Father alone who could determine the course of his life. It was his Father alone that he would trust to raise him from the dead. *That* is the example of Christ, our forerunner. You want to know "what would Jesus do?" Well, there's your best picture. He would suffer at the hands of those that should be honoring him. He would trust that this pain and death will ultimately accomplish the highest good imaginable. If you want to follow in his steps, then you will find yourself taking up a cross of your very own. You will follow him into suffering for the ones you love.

Chapter Six:

One Body on an Altar

<hr>

What is all this suffering accomplishing? Buddhists believe the purpose of life is to eliminate suffering, while the Christian faith seems to dive headlong into it. This bizarre behavior drove people like Friedrich Nietzsche to see Christianity as a sickness which must be eradicated from the world for our own good. How could anything good come from a faith founded upon loss as gain, or death as life? What purpose could all this pain and suffering serve?

The New Testament gives us numerous reasons why this part of our calling matters. Earlier, I alluded to the first reason for our own crosses. It is in losing ourselves that we truly come to know our Father well. There is a self-losing characteristic seated in the deepest reaches of his nature. Like any Father, he longs to share his nature with us. In a sense he wants to duplicate himself through a vast family of sons and daughters who will express the same kind of love toward one another. As we unite ourselves with him by losing and dying, we also come to share in his rising again. This was the cry of Paul's heart after more than twenty years of following Jesus: *"That I may know him... and the fellowship of his sufferings, being conformed to his death; in order that I may attain to the resurrection from the dead."*[1]

It is true in one sense that we have already died with him—a death to sin, Satan, the Old Man, and the present evil age. That death was accomplished once for all in the death of Christ. But there is a "working out" of this salvation which brings this spiritual reality to bear on present life experience. We must have a growing personal realization of those things which at first are merely facts on a page of the New Testament. God will provide ample opportunity for us to embrace this dying and rising again so that we may move into an experiential knowing of who he is. We move into our inheritance in him by "suffering with him so that we may also be glorified with him."[2]

All of this is done *in* the fellowship of the saints, and *for* the fellowship of the saints. Which brings me to reason number two for our suffering: *Loss for one saint means gain for another.* This is how God spreads his life. Like that grain that must fall to the ground and die in order to bear fruit, we spread his life

---

[1] Phil.3:10-11
[2] Rom.8:17

and his inheritance to others by first giving up all that we hope to gain for ourselves. "Death works in us, but life works in you," Paul said.[3] Like Paul, those called to lead the Church in this matter of suffering serve as examples for all of us. Speaking for himself, Timothy, Titus, and Silas, Paul said, "the sufferings of Christ are ours in abundance."[4] But each of us who follow Jesus has a part in shouldering this responsibility. Like Jesus before us, we too have been called to suffer for the sake of those whom we love. We connect ourselves to others and absorb their transgressions, taking them upon ourselves.

Bearing One Another

Stephen King once wrote an engrossing story called *The Green Mile*. You may have seen the film version of it. He tells of a prisoner named John Coffey, who ends up on death row for a double murder that he didn't commit. At first, the guards treat him like any other prisoner on death row. But soon they discover that John has a special gift. He can merely touch people and absorb their memories. In a flash, he takes on their past as if it were his own. But that's not all he can do. He can inhale and breathe into himself whatever illness they have. It almost kills him to take on their disease and pain, but in the end they are healed because of what he does for them. Like the gifted prisoner in King's novel, we bring life and healing through taking the sicknesses of others into ourselves. This, too, is how we walk in Christ's steps.

[3] 2 Cor.4:12
[4] 2 Cor.1:5

We are completing the task which Jesus began. "Now I rejoice in my sufferings for your sake, and in my flesh I do my share on behalf of his Body, which is the Church, in *filling up what is lacking in Christ's afflictions.*"[5] A bold statement like that should grab our attention. Filling up what is lacking in the afflictions of Christ! Did you know that Christ has not finished suffering for the sake of the Church? He continues to give himself over for her sake even now through the members of his Body. The redemption continues through us. What a calling! What a sobering thought! This is why Jesus encouraged his listeners to count the cost of following him. He made it as clear as he could that any man wanting to follow him must take up a cross of his own. All of this is done for the benefit of his Body.

Paul gives us a third reason for suffering when he explains: "We had the sentence of death within ourselves *so that we would not trust in ourselves,* but in God who raises us from the dead."[6] While he may have been talking about literal death at that moment, the same principle applies to the daily dying that we endure at our Father's hand. There is a severe mercy hidden in the slings and arrows of our misfortunes through which God intends to train us in trusting him alone. The writer of Hebrews enjoins us: "Endure hardship as discipline, for what father does not discipline his son?"[7] If the author of our salvation was

---

[5] Col.1:24
[6] 1 Cor.1:9
[7] Heb.12:7

perfected through sufferings,[8] then we should expect the same journey ahead of us as well.

Because our life grows only in degrees of dependence on his Spirit, we are at our strongest when our circumstances have reduced us to our weakest.[9] So we see that the progressive wasting away of our "outer man" (which I believe means more than just our bodies) only highlights the glory of the daily renewal of the inner man.[10] God designs these losses and failures for the destruction of our natural strengths, forcing us to trust in him alone rather than ourselves.

Finally, a fourth reason that this corporate sacrifice matters is that *God alone will receive the glory for this gospel only when the vessels which carry it are obviously not the source of its power.* "We have this treasure in earthen vessels so that the glory may not be from us."[11] Throughout the biblical narrative God has demonstrated his preference for choosing lackluster instruments for the displaying of his great power. He revels in the irony of a king born in a stable or a nation saved by a prostitute.[12] He loves to hide his mysterious ways from the wise and prudent only to reveal them to babes. It's his way of "showing off."

Sometimes the vessels he chooses still cling to the hope that they themselves will amount to something great. At those times he must deal a decisive blow to the egos in question

[8] Heb.2:10
[9] See 2 Cor.12:9
[10] 2 Cor.4:16
[11] 2 Cor.4:7
[12] Heb.11:31; Joshua 2

because he will not share his glory with another. God uses suffering because it is the best way to reveal the frailty and impotence of human flesh for producing the riches of Christ. Blessed are the poor in spirit, for they alone will inherit this kingdom.[13]

As it turns out, inheriting his kingdom comes as a direct result of sharing in the suffering of Christ. Paul says, "We are fellow heirs with Christ, if indeed we suffer with him so that we may also be glorified with him."[14] When his disciples asked him if they could rule with him in his kingdom, he replied that they must first drink the cup that he drinks. Sharing in his sufferings brings us into his invincible life by breaking down those places in ourselves that stand in the way of God's work in our hearts. As he grabs hold of those slippery remains of Adam in each of us, he makes a way for his Son to live and dwell within us. Nothing less than a cross could bring Christ into his kingdom. We should expect the same for ourselves.

Look on the Bright Side

I must add a word here about how we should view this darker side of the gospel. We must never allow ourselves to become obsessed with this aspect of our walk with God. For those who learn the importance of brokenness and loss in the life of a Christian, there comes a temptation to focus on the negative. We can easily become pessimistic or fatalistic, resigning every day to some real or imagined tragedy that

---

[13] Matt.5:3
[14] Rom.8:17

awaits us. In fact, some people will discover in themselves a near pathological *enjoyment* of anticipating pain and suffering at the hand of God. If you are one of those people, take care not to feed your natural inclination. It will not produce the fruit that you seek. You can rob yourself and those around you of the joy that is available in the midst of hardship.

Taking up your cross does not mean seeking out pain and suffering. That's not how God provides this element in our lives. You will not have to search for it – it will find you. Besides, self crucifixion never works. As a friend of mine once told me: You could nail your own feet and hand to a cross, but that other hand's still flopping around freely! Those who are naturally inclined to asceticism and self-denial will not gain any extra ground. The flesh cannot perfect itself. That's really all asceticism is. It is a peculiar kind of flesh that feels better only through self-loathing. You will find this nature well-represented in all the religions of the world. But shaved heads, self-beatings, and self-induced discomfort, poverty, and starvation do not capture the Spirit of Jesus. His Spirit is not masochistic. For him, loss is ultimately a means to some gain. Suffering with him eventually produces life and peace.

In the end, it all depends upon your perspective, doesn't it? Consider when God banished Adam and Eve from the Garden. Was that punishment or protection? It depends on how you look at it. It may be true that the Garden was a great place to live, but in what condition would they exist there? Would God allow fallen humans to eat of the Tree of Life and thereby live forever in this degenerating condition? That would not be grace. God in his mercy moved the human race out of that situation until such a time as he could provide us a way out of our predicament.

In the cross of Christ, God put an end to this old humanity. He put it in the grave. Through the resurrection of Jesus, he also provided us with a new heart and a new spirit created in the likeness of his righteous Son. This is the kind of life that can live forever in enjoyment of God. So what appeared to be God's judgment turns out to be God's salvation. We would do well to decide to trust him in those times when we do not understand his actions.

Most of God's harsh dealings in our lives need not be dark things for us. We can choose to endure hardship as discipline, because God is treating us as sons. Whether we understand it or not, it sometimes helps to remember that the trials God sends to us have an ultimately constructive purpose, either for us or for other members of the Body of Christ. We have been included in Christ. That means that God is now in us, reconciling others to himself.[15] That's good news! Once again, it all depends on how you choose to look at it.

A Higher View

Paul encourages us to step back and view our difficulties in light of the bigger picture: "I consider that the sufferings of this present time are not worthy to be compared with the glory

---

[15] 2 Cor.5:18-20

that is to be revealed to us."[16] He goes on to say that "momentary, light affliction is producing for us an eternal weight of glory far beyond all comparison, while we look not at the things which are seen, but at the things which are not seen."[17] In other words, it will greatly help us to regularly direct our attention toward those things which are our inheritance, our birthright in Christ. Take it from Paul, a brother who has earned the right to speak to us about joy in the midst of suffering. *Our burdens will weigh less on our hearts if we learn to see these events through different eyes.* We can "set our minds on things above" until we find that our minds have been renewed.[18] Our minds will be reshaped so that we see our difficulties the way God sees them.

Paul told the believers in Rome that he could "exult in tribulations" because they produce the character of Christ in us. We may draw hope from this because, in so doing, God has provided us with evidence of the presence of his Spirit in our own hearts.[19] Like a good house guest, he leaves our souls better off than he found us. We should not fail to mark these changes whenever they happen. God is giving us of his Spirit, and we will gain great ground for his name as we learn to credit him with the progress that he is making in his people. We will draw great strength and encouragement from rehearsing the ways in which God has saved us before, and is saving us still.

---

[16] Rom.8:18
[17] 2 Cor.4:17-18
[18] Col.3:1; Rom.12:2
[19] Rom.5:3-5

This encouragement moved Paul to exclaim: "If God is for us, then who can be against us?" He rattles off a litany of difficulties (distress, persecution, famine, nakedness, peril, and sword) which would seem to separate us from the caring provision of God. Then he boldly proclaims that "in all these things we overwhelmingly conquer through him."[20] If these things only draw us deeper into his life expressed on this earth, then we cannot get a bad deal no matter what happens! All of it, good and bad, accomplishes his purpose.[21] If we could soak in that light for a while each day, we would indeed look like strange people. We might find ourselves singing his praises while in chains for his testimony. Or better yet, we might even learn to *endure one another* for his name's sake!

That is the kind of sacrifice which brings a pleasant aroma before the face of God. It is a sacrifice that is corporate – the whole Body of Christ on an altar of self-spending love for one another. Isolated individuals cannot do this. It takes the whole Body of Christ. While functioning within that Body, you will find out what Jesus meant when he said, "take up your cross and follow me." When we are together in him, we will find that the path that he walks leads to an altar. But our journey will not end there. His life will not remain long in the shadow of death. He is too determined to accomplish his *eternal purpose*. It is to that very purpose that we now turn.

[20] Rom.8:31-37
[21] Thus Rom.8:28

Chapter Seven:

The Purpose of the Ages

A t this point we must step back and look at the big picture. In all this, what is God after? Where is this gospel taking us? Since it always helps to begin with the end in mind, we should ask what that end is. There is a "purpose of the ages" spoken of in the New Testament. That purpose must govern all that we do as followers of Jesus. But what is it? The answer should be emerging with each new unfolding of the good news. But before I try to spell it out, I would like to make clear what it is not.

God's ultimate goal in creating the cosmos is not salvation. Not, at least, in the way we usually envision it. Merely going to heaven doesn't fulfill God's ultimate end for us. Yet we modern evangelicals have camped out there, making the forgiveness of sins and going to heaven the primary goal of all God's interaction with us. Our hymns, our sermons, and our books reveal a centuries-old obsession with justification as an end in itself. Evangelism has become the god of today's Protestant Christianity. All things we do seem to serve that one function of the Church. Whether in Sunday School, in the Sunday morning worship service, in the pastor's sermon, or even in "prayer meeting," saving souls demands our full attention. But how can we think that's all there is?

My old pastor was a former seminary president. He once said that the only reason God doesn't take us away as soon as we're saved is that so we can stay here and get everybody else saved. I once asked another pastor what he thought would happen next if everyone got saved tomorrow. He answered that Jesus would have to come back because there would be nothing left on earth to do. That answer sounded small to me then, and I hope it strikes you the same way. I would rather know what God was aiming for when he first created…before the fall ever happened. What was he up to when he created us in the first place?

Because of their intended audience, the books of Ephesians and Colossians will give us some of the best clues. I mentioned before that Paul's letter to the Romans lays out his gospel in a way that is more comprehensive than in any of the more "situational letters." In a similar way, these two letters touch on God's larger design for creation and the cross. The letter we call "Ephesians" appears to have been intended as a circular letter[1] written for the benefit of multiple churches whom Paul had never met. In lieu of a personal visit, this letter paints a panoramic picture of God's aims for his people. From this letter, together with the help of its companion letter to the Colossians, we learn that God's "purpose of the ages" has been carefully hidden in a mystery since the first moment of creation. This is the secret which Jesus said had been kept from the wise and prudent for generations, but was now beginning to manifest itself to God's people.[2] Perhaps its mysterious nature still confounds the majority of believers, leaving us with a deficient grasp of what it's about. But Colossians unveils the mystery most succinctly: It is *Christ in y'all, the hope of glory* (please remember the "you" is plural).[3]

What is the end result of the gospel? God has been longing to inhabit this earth so that he who is invisible may be seen. He wants to be made visible in Christ and in his people. God's goal is Christ in y'all. Call it *The Incarnation, Phase Two*. The indwelling of the Spirit of Jesus has brought us into that eternal stream of God's purpose in creation. Our all-consuming task is to give expression to his nature on this earth now, not merely one day when we reach heaven. In fact, the New Testament says very little about God bringing us to some other place. At its most climactic moments, God's revelation to us speaks of *the heavens coming here*. We've been preoccupied with

---

[1] Our earliest copies of the letter don't include "at Ephesus" in the greeting.

[2] Mt. 11:25

[3] Col.1:27

"getting to heaven." God himself seems more intent on coming to earth! As we take the time to look at this intention, we will see that this purpose reaches all the way back to the beginning of creation.

Back to the Garden

The biblical narrative begins with a man in a garden. This garden is special because it represents the meeting place between God and Man. They would walk together 'in the cool of the day" and Adam could hear God speak. It was there that Adam and Eve learned that they were to be fruitful and multiply, filling the earth and subduing it. They were to build a family and rule over the earth as God rules over all of creation. In this place, they could learn how to do what it was that they were created to do.

In this garden, two images of God's purpose emerged. First, the Lord made a bride with whom the man may share his responsibility in filling and subduing the earth. In order to provide the man with this, God put him under a deep sleep and extracted a portion of the man's own side. God then "built" that portion into a woman for him and presented her to him. Adam exclaimed that she was "bone of [his] bone and flesh of [his] flesh."[4] He was most impressed by the fact that this lovely creature was made from his own self. How could he not love one that was so much a part of himself?

---

[4] Gen.2:23

Genesis instructs us that this beautiful relationship is to be re-enacted time and again in marriage. Each successive generation of mankind can celebrate this arrangement whenever a man "leaves his father and mother to be joined to his wife, becoming one flesh with her."[5] This uniting signifies the oneness of identity that the first man and woman shared. But as Paul would later reveal, even this relationship illustrates something much larger than that. This arrangement pictures something so powerful and multifaceted that its form will change from time to time in order to express its purpose. Before we follow that trail, we must notice one other charge that God gave humanity at the outset of this drama.

The man and his wife were to eat from the Tree of Life. Whatever this tree signifies, it must carry great meaning for God's purpose of the ages. In this tree we find tangible fruit which offers us something not of this world. It represents a physical manifestation of eternal life.[6] As strange as that sounds, we will later hear of something very similar when Jesus describes himself as a Vine in which we are the branches, bearing his fruit. This Vine/Tree is unique in that it results from the mingling of two realms. The Tree of Life represents an intrusion of the heavenly realm into the earthly one. Here in the fruit of this Tree you can sample the produce of the invisible realm. The invisible becomes partake-able. That is part of God's purpose as well.

---

[5] Gen.2:24
[6] Gen.3:22

ow God's authority and image could multiply, fill the earth, and subdue it. But our predecessors failed to take hold of that honor. They fell short of the glory of God. Their story illustrates the legacy that all mankind has maintained since the beginning of our species. We were meant for the glory of God, but we missed the mark.

It is ironic that Genesis says "their eyes were opened." In reality we became blind to so many things from that moment on. Fallen humanity was plunged into a profound darkness which prevents us from seeing our own hearts. This darkness blinds us to the things that are most important in life, so that our priorities are forever upside down and inside out. We spend our lives chasing after shadows that seem to offer us the things that we need – the glory we are meant for – but in the end they are all cheap imitations.

It was in grace that God expelled mankind from that garden so that we would not partake of life eternal while still in this wretched state. Living forever like this would be cruel punishment indeed. God would not allow it for his children. Thus he began the long period of instruction for his people. With unimaginable patience, he set out to teach us to recognize our condition. With every trial and tribulation, every war and famine and disaster, and finally with the giving of the Law itself through Moses, God hammered home to us our need for rescue from our fallen situation. With object lessons and great dramatic imagery, God surrounded his people with "rumors of another world,"[7] hinting to us that life can be restored to its intended design and beauty.

A Haunting Mystery

The long journey to fulfillment began when Abraham became haunted by dream of a land and a city for those who call on the name of the Lord.[8] God also promised him that a large family would come from his own aged body and from Sarah's barren womb. God promised him a seed, and Abraham believed him, although he didn't fully understand how God would make it happen. A new race of people was born that day, even though the physical descendants of Abraham would one day fall away from that faith which distinguished him from all other people. The basic elements of God's purpose were there in this man's heart from the beginning: An abundant land flowing with milk and honey, a seed that would become a vast family, a nation with God as their only authority, and a city whose architect and builder is God. In other words, *he was looking for a place where God and Man could live together again.*

Over time, this haunting dream would change shape to express different sides of God's intention for his people. Like an object with an irregular shape, it looks like something different

---

[7] Philip Yancey wrote a book by this title, exploring God's hidden messages in creation (Grand Rapids: Zondervan, 2003).
[8] Heb.11:8-10

each way you turn it. In the days of Moses, it appeared in the form of a tabernacle. This elaborate tent provided a meeting place on earth for God and Man, and it took up far more attention in the Law that any other single thing. In time, that "building" which did not yet have foundations would become the center of Israel's life.

Another man haunted by this dream was David. He was called a man after God's own heart. But why? It was because he was consumed with zeal for the house of God. He burned with a passion to see God at home on the earth, although like Abraham he misperceived the form that this mystery would take. He chose to enshrine God's residence on earth with a temple made of stone. This project missed God's original intent,[9] but God eventually honored David's dream and promised an eternal kingdom to his posterity.

The visions didn't stop there, though. Jeremiah spoke of a riddle which no one in the days of the old covenant understood. He prophesied that the Lord would create "a new thing on the earth: a woman will encompass a man."[10] For Jeremiah, *the house had become a woman.* God had loved Israel as a husband would his wife, but she did not return his love.[11] Her unfaithfulness to his covenant provoked him to make a new covenant which would ensure better results. Under his new

---

[9] 2 Sam.7:5-7
[10] Jer.31:22
[11] Jer.31:32

covenant his bride would not be satisfied by anything less than her true Lover.

Hosea had encountered this same image when God told him to marry a prostitute. This poor man learned what it felt like to love a woman who would not be faithful in return. Each time Hosea restored Gomer, she turned again to run after other lovers. But God declared that he would yet win *his* beloved to himself. He promised that he would one day lure her into the wilderness (remember that) and speak kindly to her.[12] He would make his new covenant with her and betroth her to himself forever. Only this time, he would call on those who had not been his people before.[13] A new people would make up his betrothed, and they would truly know him.

Isaiah dreamed of a *holy mountain* upon which God and man would meet and share life. He called it Zion and professed its glory and importance like a man obsessed. In Ezekiel's line of sight the mystery morphed back into a temple, only this time the Holiest Place (the square portion wherein God dwelt) had engulfed the whole temple! Just as that first Garden had been watered by rivers, so this temple had rivers of living water flowing out from it, producing groves of fruit-bearing trees. Most importantly, the name of this place was called "The Lord is there."[14]

These are the visions which wove themselves into the

[12] Hosea 2:14
[13] Hosea 2:18-20, 23
[14] Ezek.48:35

collective consciousness of God's people for centuries until the time of fulfillment had finally come. Few could connect them because they seemed like separate things. Invariably, God's people misunderstood his intent. They supposed that God was after something geopolitical. Some are fighting for it still today. What they fail to see is that Christ showed up and clarified the true nature of the purpose of God.

The Dream Fulfilled

One day the Mystery decided to peek through the curtain, showing only his head. According to John's gospel, this one for whom all the earth had been waiting chose to make his presence known first at a wedding, even though it was not his own.[15] Surely this revealed something important about the fulfillment of God's purpose. This long awaited one had come, himself in expectation, to claim for himself a bride. The fourth gospel reports that when Jesus first appeared before his people, his cousin John announced his coming *in the wilderness*. John introduced himself as merely the friend of the Bridegroom, who had finally come for his betrothed.

When Jesus began his teaching ministry, however, he did not at first speak of a bride for himself. He chose instead to speak about that kingdom that God had promised to David long before. Never actually defining what that kingdom was, Jesus announced the good news that the time for the kingdom had come. In him, the human race could regain access into that

---

[15] John 2:1-10

joining of heaven and earth which God had intended from the beginning. Once this kingdom had come, God's will would be done on earth as easily as it is done in heaven.[16]

We must realize that much of what Jesus had to say was lost on his original audience. Their utter lack of comprehension led him to limit his public speaking to riddles and parables about the kingdom. Ironically, people still love to say that Jesus told parables because "stories are so helpful." But Jesus himself said that these worked more to conceal than to reveal their mysterious meanings.[17] I have a notion that this may be why the first three gospels (Matthew, Mark, and Luke) paint such a different picture of Jesus' spoken ministry than the one we find in John's gospel. Perhaps the first three make use of the public words and works of Jesus, while the fourth gospel gives us the more intimate "behind the scenes" look that the other gospels missed.[18] Jesus eventually admitted that he had many more things that he wanted to say to them, but that these would have to wait until *something else* arrived on the scene.[19]

What he did not conceal was his zeal for the house of God. He shocked everyone by tearing through the Temple courtyard with an improvised whip, driving the merchants from their profitable trade. He then declared that if anyone destroyed the Temple of God, he would raise it up on the third day. His

---

[16] Matt.6:10
[17] Mk.4:10-12
[18] Craig Blomberg suggests this in his *Historical Reliability of the Gospels* (Downers Grove: InterVarsity, 1987), p.184-185.
[19] John 16:12-13

behavior and his words perplexed those who heard him. He further confused them when he confided to his disciples that he was really speaking of his own body. Who exactly is this man and for what has he come? For a bride or a temple? And what did his body have to do with any of this? How could he speak interchangeably about so many different things, *unless they are not different things at all*? While God had spoken to our forefathers in a piecemeal fashion, in symbols and types and figures, he was now ready to open the floodgates of Heaven through his Son.[20]

But first he would have to be placed into the ground like a grain of wheat in order to increase and come out again as an entire harvest. Like the first Adam, he would have to fall under a "deep sleep" so that his Father could pierce his side, giving birth to something the world had been awaiting since it first came into being. It was time for the rest of the mystery to be unveiled. It was time for the Spirit of God to bring together the Church of God.

When the Church first appeared in Jerusalem, no one knew what to call it. This unnatural colony defied all categorization. Here was a group of people, loving one another, sharing each others' lives, and speaking with such power and authority! Even demons and diseases obeyed their commands! It was as if the true masters of the house had finally returned from a long journey and were ready to set the house in order. The world had seen this kind of life before in Jesus, but now it

---

[20] Heb.1:1-2

had multiplied and spread. Ungodly men quickly learned to hate these people because their open, authentic character stood in sharp contrast to their own wicked self-interests. These bothersome "little Christs" walked the streets like brilliant lights, exposing every hidden motive and practice in the world around them. This kind of light was not welcome. But whenever one was put out, five others would ignite in its stead. This unquenchable fire was not native to this fallen earth; but here it was, right in the center of the human race. Thus began the unveiling of God's hidden plans for this creation.

Paul would spend scroll after scroll trying to give utterance to the gift that has been given to us in Christ and in his Church. Suddenly all of the images and metaphors of God's purpose have converged on this one entity. The Church embodies that house, that mountain, that family, that kingdom, and that bride for which all of creation was purposed. Paul also spoke of the Church as the Body of Christ, the Preeminent One. In so doing, he gave us a common function and an equal status to that of our Head. He implored us to lay hold of our place in God's design for creation. With every new difficulty that challenged the churches, Paul would write to them to heighten and deepen their understanding of what had been given them in Christ. In other words, he wrote *to increase their faith.*

The Torah had long before taught that "the righteous will live by faith." Now in the story of the early Church we learn what that faith looks like. Faith lies at the heart of Jesus' call to follow him. So it is upon faith that this kingdom is built. Let us consider for a moment what this faith means.

Chapter Eight:

The Substance of Things Hoped For

J esus loved to say, "Your faith has made you well." He often made a point of saying that after he healed someone. His highest praise was reserved for people like the centurion who said that Jesus only needed to say the word, and it would be done. The centurion understood who Jesus was and he understood that Jesus had authority over everything. Jesus responded by exclaiming that he had not found such great faith in all of Israel. He was rarely impressed, so we should take note of it when it happens.

In this adventure we are on, it is our grasp of who Christ is, and of who we are in him, that determines our level of involvement in his work. If you will examine Paul's letters to the churches, you will find that the majority of each letter is occupied with revealing the glory of Christ rather than directly addressing the problems faced by each church. Granted, Paul eventually tells them what to do in order to deal with their problems. But first he always takes the opportunity to unfold the majesty and the exaltation of the person and work of Christ on our behalf. Paul expects that our "getting" who Christ is will make the needed changes in our hearts. He eventually adds his more practical instructions on the end of each letter, but they almost appear as an afterthought.

Ironically, ministers preaching from the traditional pulpit draw most of their sermon material from these smaller end-caps of Paul's letters. They do this because they do not understand the depths and heights available to us in the "meatier" portions of the letters. At every turn, Paul's instructions for the Church stem directly from some aspect of who Christ is. Like one of my seminary professors would always say: The *imperatives* of our faith are founded upon the great *indicatives* of who Christ is, and of what he has accomplished. I wish every minister could have been exposed to a truth like that before being unleashed on their congregations.

Take sexual promiscuity, for example. When Paul learned that some believers in Corinth were still regularly seeing prostitutes (a common cultural norm in the city at that time), he didn't simply tell them, "Don't do that!" He wrote to them and reminded them that they had joined themselves to Christ so that they were one spirit with him.[1] They had personally become

---

[1] 1 Cor.6:17

temples of God's Spirit, carrying him around with them wherever they went and in whatever they did. So when they used the services of one of these women, they were in effect joining Jesus Christ to a prostitute.

Wow. Forget for a moment that you've been told since you were little that "your body is a temple." Probably you heard it as an argument to exercise or to eat your green beans or something like that. What a powerful pronouncement to make! Walking in that kind of awareness of the presence of God's Spirit, how could anyone continue living like a typical Corinthian? A truth like that has the power to alter the way we think about everything.

It was for this transformation of our minds that Paul was aiming whenever he wrote to the churches that he established.

> My prayer for you is that the eyes of your heart may be enlightened, so that you will know what is the hope of his calling, what are the riches of the glory of his inheritance in the saints, and what is the surpassing greatness of his power toward us who believe.[2]

This encapsulates the heart of the mystery which we have been exploring. As members of the risen, reigning Christ, we are buoyed above the despair and self-destructiveness of the fallen world around us. When our minds are renewed by news this good, everything else about us is affected. We must see that all the treasures of wisdom and knowledge are hidden in Christ himself.[3] What we are after is not merely serving Christ, but

---

[2] Eph.1:18-19
[3] Col.2:3

partaking of him as our supply for everything that we need. To find our completeness in him is our goal.

And not just me, the individual. *We* will lay hold of him as *our* inheritance, *our* endless supply of wealth and riches in the heavenly realms. Somehow we must see that we are sitting on a vast ocean of value and power, and that we need only know him as ours in order to see his greatness manifested in our very own bodies.

The Growing Christ

The other prayer that Paul offered in Ephesians asked that God would use the unsearchable riches of Christ to empower us "through his Spirit in the inner man, so that Christ may dwell in [our] hearts through faith."[4] We know that his Spirit already has been given to us "as a pledge of our inheritance"[5] and that through this Spirit Christ already indwells us. But Paul is pointing to something bigger here. As our faith—our heart's grasp of who Christ is in us—grows, he comes to take up a more evident presence in our midst as a people.

Writing to pull the Galatians out of their legalistic mire, Paul intimates that he was "in labor again until Christ is formed in you."[6] Like most places in the New Testament, that "you" is plural. So a more precise way to put that would be "until Christ

---

[4] Eph.3:14-17
[5] Eph.1:14
[6] Gal.4:19

is formed *among y'all.*" Do you see what he's getting at? The resurrected Christ desires to continue his unfolding of God's self-expression through the whole Church. That's why we exist. That's why we meet. That's the purpose behind everything that happens around us. Every trial, every victory, every defeat, every pressure, and every joy feeds into this one end: the revealing of the sons of God.[7]

This high purpose becomes our present reality as we come to see more clearly who he is *to us* (he is our all) and who he is *in us* (he is our new identity as a people). As he increases our awareness of this good news, the New Man grows and matures before our very eyes. The risen Christ appears in corporate manifestation, showing his nature and love through our actions and our words. No part of him will be left unrepresented. As we speak these truths to one another, we will ultimately grow up as a people into the fullness of who he is.[8] We can expect nothing less than the full measure of the stature of Christ lived out in our own hearts.

Oh, What a Foretaste (of Glory Divine)

Something new is starting to appear on this earth. The world as we know it may "stink" sometimes, but something better is coming. There is a new reality gradually dawning in the midst of "this present evil age"[9] and this growing light hints

---

[7] Rom.8:19
[8] Eph.4:12-16
[9] Gal.1:4

at our future glory. We are part of a coming kingdom that is so big that it is both already here and yet still coming.

When Jesus healed, he often made two statements about what he was doing. When they asked him how he did it, he would say that their faith had made them well. And when they asked him what these signs meant, he told them the kingdom of God had come. His emphasis on their faith should impress upon us how central to our lives faith is, and how instrumental it is to the coming of the kingdom. Faith is not merely the prerequisite for entering that kingdom. It is the ongoing means for bringing Christ into this fallen existence, from start to finish. Our faith in God's revelation concerning his Son connects us with a reality that seems like it shouldn't yet be available to us. But what is *time* to the sons of God, anyway?

In fact, you will not long read the New Testament before you notice a tension between the present and the future in everything it asserts. Sometimes the writers say that something is true now, only to turn around and say that it will be true someday in the future. It's like they couldn't make up their minds whether these things were already true now, or not yet. Theologians understandably call this the tension of "the already and the not yet." Unfortunately, this little formula too often gives people an excuse for dismissing things that seem too hard to believe.

When some read that they have been given the very righteousness of Christ, they conclude that this new state will not have much real effect on them until the end of the ages has come and their bodies are redeemed. The paradox is that this is true in a way, but in another sense it is not. First of all, it is true that somehow the possession of these fallen bodies is connected with the presence of evil in our lives.[10] We will not be totally free of sin's influence until something dramatic is done to remedy our physical condition. We have a reliable word from God that a change is coming one day which will bring the redemption of our very bodies,[11] thus rescuing us from this "wretched" state in which we often find ourselves.

It was to prove this point that Jesus healed people, showing them that wholeness is coming to these messed up carcasses that we carry around. He offered his greatest proof when he rose from the grave, demonstrating for us that even death has been defeated in the cross. That great moment gives us the assurance that we, too, will not remain in the grave. The same power that raised him from the dead will raise us, too, and we can fix our hope on that.

But we do not have to wait until we die to see this kingdom starting to grow. The hope of future grace is not all that he gives us. God has even now given us his Spirit in our hearts as a pledge of our inheritance.[12] In other words, Christ in us is already our "hope of glory,"[13] our assurance of better

---

[10] This is not to say that matter is somehow inherently evil. That belief originated with Gnosticism and Neoplatonism, not with the Christian faith.

[11] Rom.8:23

[12] Eph.1:14

[13] Col. 1:27

CHRIST IN Y'ALL | 119

things to come. Those of us who were not physically present at the tomb of Jesus have more to go on than just the word of a handful of people who saw him alive from the dead. If that were all we had then we would have been a pitiful little movement indeed. Instead, his presence manifests itself in our midst today, giving palpable evidence to a greater anticipation still headed our way.

A Timeless Perspective

I have always been a sucker for movies about time travel. *Back to the Future, Time Bandits, The Terminator, Peggy Sue Got Married, The Time Machine, 12 Monkeys* – if it has anything to do with time travel, I'll watch it and probably love it. Something about that possibility fascinates me. C.S. Lewis said that it's a clue to our immortal destinies that we are always feeling constrained by time. We are always surprised by its passing. Modern physics has gone so far as to question the notion that time moves only in one direction. Einstein's model of space and time suggests that time itself isn't so constant or immovable as we have always understood it. Maybe that's why so many movies today play around with the distortion of time. Deep down we know that we should be free from its constraints.

I believe it was also Lewis who used a parade to illustrate the limitations of our perception of time. To alter his illustration a bit, imagine watching the Macy's Thanksgiving Day parade from Harold Square. The parade begins with huge inflatable stars, tethered to dozens of volunteers on the ground.

You stand and watch for hours as the boisterous parade slowly makes its way across the square, balloon by balloon and float by float. When the parade comes to its conclusion, you'll see Santa Claus pull up in the end, ushering in the official beginning of the Christmas season. Lewis suggests that there is another way to experience a parade like this one. You could stand on top of the tallest building (or today you could get in a helicopter and fly above Manhattan), viewing the whole parade in an instant. In the front of the line you'll see the stars and the rest of the floats. Looking down toward the end you'll see Santa making his way toward his final destination. You can experience the whole parade at once! It's the same parade, only your frame of reference has changed.

Maybe God transcends time and history in the same way. That would explain why his comments are so puzzling. When Moses asked for God's name, God replied, "I AM."[14] This unusual name signifies a Presence that simultaneously occupies the past, the present, and the future. The beasts in the book of Revelation worship at his feet, calling him the One who is, and who was, and who is to come.[15] Like the pilot of that helicopter over the Macy's parade, God does not experience time in the same way that we do. Whose perception do you suppose is right, and whose is off? We will have to get used to hearing things from his perspective from now on.

---

[14] Exod.3:14
[15] Rev.4:8

Dead Men Walking

Listen to some of the things that Paul says passed away in the cross:

- *Our old self was crucified with him* in order that our body of sin might be done away with, so that we would no longer be slaves to sin; for he who has died is freed from sin (Rom.6:6-7).
- Those who belong to Christ Jesus *have crucified the flesh* with its passions and desires (Gal.5:24).
- *You were made to die* to the Law through the body of Christ (Rom.7:4).
- Having been buried with him… you were also raised up with him… *having cancelled out the certificate of debt consisting in decrees* against us… he has taken it out of the way, having nailed it to the cross (Col.2:11ff).
- Through the cross of Christ *the world has been crucified to me, and I to the world* (Gal.6:14).

That pretty much covers everything, doesn't it? Christ did not go to the grave empty handed. That grave was a large grave indeed. In it were sin, the flesh, the Law, death, and even *you*. He had said that if he be lifted up he would draw "all" to himself. He didn't specify: All what? All people? All things? All principalities and powers? If we could see the cross through the eyes of God, we would see that the entire old creation passed away in that incredible cross. *The world has been crucified to me, and I to the world.*

Something unique happened in the crucifixion of Jesus. That death and resurrection did not merely occupy that one point in time. It seems that at that point in time *something eternal intersected with time.* We simply got to see it for the first time on that day outside of Jerusalem. This slain Lamb predated everything else that had transpired until that moment. Not only that, but he continues in our midst even now. He will also be celebrated in the end when all are gathered around his throne, singing "worthy is the Lamb who was slain to receive power and riches and wisdom and might and honor and glory and blessing."[16] We who live in the 21st century are in no way separated from that cross or that Christ. Somehow they are the ground of existence for all history and all time.

Our natural minds don't get this at all, do they? We understand a man dying and being buried in a tomb. We can even understand that he arose from the grave after he died. But what's this about *us dying with him*? And how could anyone say that all those things passed away with him, too? It certainly doesn't look like they did. Sin, the flesh, the Law, and death seem to be alive and well to this day. We struggle with them on a daily basis, don't we?

Here is where we begin to learn what it feels like to live by faith and not by sight. We have stumbled upon a profound paradox. As believers in Christ we straddle two worlds. Two opposing realities cross paths inside of our own hearts, leaving us perplexed at ourselves. We can't figure out if we're sinners or saints. The one thing that we know is that things do not appear to have changed since the death and resurrection of

---

[16] Rev.5:12

Jesus. The world keeps steadily marching toward its ultimate demise, and we seem to be going down with it.

But wait a minute. Something else is going on, too. We have awakened to another reality that we cannot deny. Internally, we have tasted and smelled and heard something that didn't come from this world. Others around us may not have any idea what we're talking about, but we know it to be true. It runs deeper than what we see with our natural eyes. It is a new creation, and it has taken root in our hearts. It grows little by little as we learn to acknowledge its presence in our lives.

Walking By Faith

We start by believing what God says about us. Never mind the conflicting signals that we so often get. We are *believers*. We instinctively cling to his words, don't we? Don't we find that our first response to the gospel is one of acceptance and trust? That is what we do. That's how we're made.

I think this is why Jesus said that the citizens of the kingdom of God are like little children. My children naturally believe everything I tell them. I could tell them that the earth spins on top of a giant panda and they would at first believe me. I'm their father. What a powerful yet humbling responsibility I have as a parent! Little children naturally trust those who care for them. In the same way, we instinctively trust our Father in heaven. To move forward from here, we simply need to recognize those instincts and learn to live by them.

Paul says we must "reckon" ourselves as crucified with Christ.[17] After hearing the word of this good news, we decide to count on it as true whether we see it in our immediate experience or not. We can choose to live as if we really have been released from the world's power. Paul calls this "presenting" ourselves to God as dead to sin and alive to him.[18] C.S. Lewis calls it "dressing up as Christ."[19] Lewis instructs us: "Do not waste your time bothering whether you 'love' your neighbour; act as if you did."[20]

Through the daily practice of our faith, the Holy Spirit will make the objective truths of the New Testament real in our subjective experience. Of course, we won't be able to dissect where God's work ends and our work begins. They are inexplicably interwoven as one. But we need not worry about any apparent contradiction between God's sovereignty and our own human effort. While theologians and philosophers argue about which one comes first, Paul simply assumes they go hand in hand. With fear and trembling, we work out a salvation that grows according to His sovereign working within us.[21]

Watchman Nee described this process by pulling out the three main three verbs of Romans six: knowing, reckoning, and presenting. Our first step is to learn what has happened in the death and resurrection of Jesus. We must first *hear* the good

[17] Rom.6:11
[18] Rom.6:13
[19] Lewis, p.161.
[20] Ibid., p.116.
[21] Phil.2:13

news if we are going to believe it. Next, we count on it as true (that's reckoning). We take him at his word and choose to live as if nothing else *could* be true. Then comes presenting ourselves to God as ones no longer tied to the self-love of the old humanity. We will face daily persuasion to the contrary, so this will take the rest of our lives to get used to.

It will come in handy to have other believers with whom you may embark on this journey. This was never meant to be done alone. With the whole world against you, *you will need the help of others who can remind you of what is true.* You will need their encouragement on a daily basis. Those who ignore this need may very well end their journey in disappointment.

Walking by faith begins with knowing that the cross changed everything. Without that knowledge, we will be building our houses on the shifting sand of the old humanity. It's hard to define what the alternative looks like; but a life built on the solid rock of Christ doesn't require as much strain. It's not a sprint or a climb. It is a walk. When a soul has learned to see the world through these new eyes, the Christian life becomes as natural as putting one foot in front of the other.

A New Man

Permit me one more illustration about time. Imagine now that the entire creation from beginning to end was captured on a single film strip. Each frame of the strip represents the entire universe at this moment, then the next moment, and then the next, and so on. Of course, a film strip is only two dimensional. So imagine instead that this movie strip has three dimensions. Each frame has length, width, and depth to it. Can you picture that? Each frame of history contains the entire universe. Once it is viewed all together it forms a panoramic record of time and space, from its creation to its consummation. All of history living inside a very long, very large film strip.

We watch this movie one frame at a time. Each image passes in front of us one at a time (or maybe we pass through each frame) until our place in the movie fades away. The way we see the movie, Christ and his cross occupy a small portion of the movie. Their part occurred in a different place, separated from us by thousands of years. But how does God experience this story? Obviously I cannot say with much certainty. But I can imagine one possibility....

Remove time from this film strip. That's right; just suck it out of the equation and see what happens. Our filmstrip collapses into one large frame. In this huge frame you will find everything that ever transpired—only it's all happening at once. The first moment is not distinct from the last, or from anything in between. The cross is no longer separate from the beginning or the end. The human race is no longer an innumerable mass of scattered persons, separated by generations or centuries. They are all connected like one long stream of humanity. Now remove "space" from the equation as well, and what happens? All creation, all activity, and all humanity collapse into one... Man! One. Big. Man.

Technically, if you look closer, you'll see *two* men there, with one inside the other. One is Adam (a.k.a. the Old Man), and he is crucified and buried within the other. The other is Christ, the New Man. These two men are *corporate* men. By that I mean that each one consists of an entire race of men and women. I think this resembles the way God sees humanity. Every man, woman, and child is either "in Adam" or "in Christ," and the old humanity has its end in the new. Can you see how humanity is all connected? All of us born into the old creation were born "in Adam." His fall was our fall. God sees us as one organism.

Christ's cross and his death encompass everything – all time, all space, all creation. The old creation met its end in this cross. In a way that cannot yet be seen by everyone, the entire old creation passed away with him. A new one began *in him*. He himself is a new creation, an alternate universe in whom all things are reconciled to God. In this universe—in him—Satan has been destroyed. Sin has been eliminated. Guilt has been erased. Death itself has met its own death in the death of Christ.[22]

They Shall See God

Tozer said that "faith is the gaze of a soul upon a saving God."[23] Our hearts can see with eyes made for invisible things.

---

[22] For this sentence I am indebted to John Owen's clever title *The Death of Death* (Edinburgh: Banner of Truth, 1959).

[23] Tozer, p.89.

Our eyes and our minds will tell us that this creation certainly has *not* ended. As you look around right now you will see that it appears that the old creation is alive and well (or sick and dying, as the case may be). Your daily life demands that you attend to this creation as if it were the only one in existence.

But there is a kingdom coming. You have seen it. You have tasted it. The very light and life that sometimes bubble up inside you testify to its coming. You are the firstfruits of this new creation[24]; and not you alone, but you together with all those who have died and risen again with him. Together, we are God's announcement that something new, something wonderful, has broken in upon this old world. It is Christ in y'all, the hope of glory.

Like the Tree that was in the garden, giving spiritual life in an earthly form, we bear the fruit of another realm. That fruit proves that what he said is true. What does that fruit look like, you ask? It looks like things that have become familiar to so many believers, but may look very strange to those rooted only in earthly places. It looks like joy in the midst of difficulty, peace in the midst of a storm, patience in the face of mistreatment, and gentleness in response to wrath. All these grow naturally from the Vine which connects the "not yet" kingdom to our "already" lives. These things are natural to the life of Christ, who has taken up residence in our hearts. We sometimes forget what treasures we have, and *that is why the preaching of the unsearchable riches of Christ means so much to God's*

---

[24] Rom.8:23

people. It is our faith that makes us whole, and faith comes by hearing the word of God spoken among us (more on that in Chapter Ten).

As we hear the good news of the unfathomable riches of Christ proclaimed, Christ grows among us until his nature has taken over every part of our lives. Through his Spirit inside us, Christ increasingly dwells in our hearts so that we may begin to grasp *together with all the saints* what is the immense height and depth and breadth of the love of Christ.[25] We begin to grasp it because his loving nature begins to permeate our own hearts until we love one another by the same love with which he loves us. Above all other fruits and evidences of that other realm, love ranks the most important. Love is the chief character trait of God. Therefore our love gives the most powerful testimony of his presence in our hearts. God's people will be known by their love for one another. When God gets what he's after, his house will be known as a house of love.

---

[25] Eph.3:16-19

Chapter Nine:

A House of Love

W hat does a healthy church look like? What characterizes a church that is growing and maturing along the lines of God's heart? Perhaps another way to ask the same question would be: What is the end result, in practical terms, of God's eternal purpose working amongst a group of people? I believe real-life examples of healthy churches are diverse beyond what we can imagine since the unsearchable riches of Christ could never be expressed entirely by any one group of people at any given time. In fact, I think the expression of God's nature through the Church must be viewed globally and timelessly. It takes *all the saints* (not merely those confined to one place and time) to grasp the fullness of Christ.[1] His Body's many members will not always look alike in form or function.

---

[1] Eph.3:18-19

But I do know one central trait which will always identify those churches who are being filled with his life: they love one another.

Some teachers of the Law in Jesus' day were fond of boiling the many laws in the Old Testament down to two: Love God and love one another.[2] For once, Jesus himself seemed to agree with them. This simplification of the Torah frames his teaching so completely that Scot McKnight calls this the *Jesus Creed*.[3] Without love at the core, our actions would be vain religious duty. Everything in our relationship with God stems from loving him, and everything in our relationship with each other issues from loving one another.

One day, a young man asked Jesus what he thought was the most important commandment. Jesus quoted the popular pairing, adding that the second "is just like" the first. I used to wonder what he meant by that. Then it occurred to me that, from God's perspective, loving one another *is* loving God. It's like Jesus combines our vertical relationship to God with our horizontal relationship to each other. As John put it: "If someone says 'I love God' and hates his brother, he is a liar... whoever loves the Father loves the child born of him."[4]

See if you can follow this progression: Jesus told us that if we love him, we will obey his commandments.[5] John repeated

---

[2] Matt.22:36-40
[3] Scot McKnight, *The Jesus Creed* (Brewster: Paraclete, 2004).
[4] 1 Jn.4:20; 5:1
[5] John 14:15

that statement later when he said "this is the love of God, that we keep his commandments; and his commandments are not burdensome."[6]   So loving God equals obeying his commandments, and whatever those commandments are, they will not be overwhelming like the old ones were.[7] Unlike the Law of Moses, his yoke is easy and his burden is really no burden at all. Fortunately, we are not left guessing what his command is: "This is his commandment, that we believe in the name of his Son, Jesus Christ, and love one another."[8]

I don't know if that counts as two commandments or one, but later he shortens it again to one: "The one who loves God should love his brother also."[9] The first requirement really summarizes the foundation of our faith in Christ. We believe in him. Got it. Check! This means that loving one another is all we have left to do. What utter simplicity! There is only one rule in the house of God: Love one another. That's it. How simple is that?

It cannot be overstated here that this love for one another finds its source in our love for God himself.   Dietrich Bonhoeffer's words should drive this point hard into our minds:

> There is a human love of one's neighbor...Human love is directed to the other person for his own sake, spiritual love loves him for Christ's sake.[10]

---

[6] 1 Jn.5:3

[7] Acts 15:10

[8] 1 Jn.3:23

[9] 1 Jn.4:21

[10] Dietrich Bonhoeffer, *Life Together* (New York: Harper & Row), pp.33-34.

We must drink deeply of the knowledge that our natural selves chase after community for ultimately self-serving reasons. This is not what God seeks to establish. This kind of love issues from his own heart, and it can never be manufactured by even the sincerest intentions. We love with the love we have received from our Father in heaven.

A *New* Commandment?

Our love for God finds its most natural outlet in loving one another. "A new commandment I give to you, that you love one another even as I have loved you...by this everyone will know that you are my disciples."[11] How could he say that this is new? Wasn't this the second of the two greatest commandments from the beginning? I see two or three reasons why this is new.

First of all, this is new because from *this point on, everything is new!* The slate has been wiped clean and a new relationship between God and his people has begun. In this new covenant, all of God's instructions for his children have consolidated into one: Love one another. We were never that good at remembering so many different requirements anyway. Who could ever keep up with 613 instructions? God has streamlined his directions for the Church to this one thing. We are to take care of one another just as a loving family does.

Perhaps another thing that is new here is that, rather than codifying our conduct with specific rules and expectations,

---

[11] John 13:34 (NRSV)

God is directing our hearts to the Spirit behind the Law. *Why* did he say not to steal from one another? Because stealing hurts your brother. *Why* did he tell us not to lie? Because your sister needs to know the truth. *Why* must we not murder? Because the life that you take is precious. Come to think of it, even hating your brother does a kind of damage, and that falls short of loving him as well. That is what Jesus was driving home to his followers in his "sermon on the mount." He clarified beautifully that it's not always about whether or not you engage in one specific behavior or another. What matters most is the spirit in which you act. What matters is what's happening on the inside.

Our flesh will always demand a list to live by, with boundaries and rules clearly spelled out for us. But the Spirit of Jesus will not be so easily boxed in. You cannot always predict what he will do. What you can be sure of is *what makes him act.* He wants what will benefit his people. The means to that end may look strange or even wrong sometimes, but that is how he operates. And it drives religious people crazy. The Spirit whom God has put inside us is alive, active, and able to lead us. He will enable us to love as we have been called to love, moment by moment, case by case.

Take the matter of alcohol for example. What is God's desire about "drinking"? Is it right or wrong? The old way of answering that question is to approach the Bible like a rulebook. You simply scour the pages until you find verses which describe wine as a mocker. Maybe you find the Nazarite vow which rules out wine and conclude that drinking is wrong. Anyone who does it is therefore sinning and should be corrected. On the other hand, you may read about Jesus turning water into wine at a wedding or serving wine to his disciples at the Last Supper. That may lead you to conclude that there's nothing wrong with it. Your rule then becomes that you *should* be able to drink. Anyone who says you can't is putting God's people under Law.

Paul took the matter to higher ground when he said that "the kingdom of God is not about eating and drinking."[12] What matters most is that we love one another, being sensitive to the leading of the Spirit within us. Does becoming a teetotaler help you love your brothers and sisters? If the answer is "no," then for crying out loud, have a beer! On the other hand, if drinking in your situation means that a brother or sister is harmed in some way, then by all means don't do it. Loving one another will not always look identical in every situation. In the end, it's about internal things that you can't reduce to a static code of conduct. When compared to the old way of computing "righteousness," this kind of love goes deeper and farther than the natural human mind would ever understand. It requires utter dependence on the Lord.

Jesus showed us a new *kind* of love. That is the third reason why he called this a new commandment. In the past, we heard that we were to love our neighbor as ourselves. But this new standard compels us to love one another as *he* loves, and that's a qualitative leap. It's a different sort of love by far. He

---

[12] Rom. 14:17

said that the kind of righteousness exhibited by citizens of the kingdom of God would exceed the righteousness of the scribes and Pharisees. Indeed it does, for this new kind of life lays down its own needs for the needs of another, even if that "other" happens to be an enemy! As Jesus rinsed the dirty toes of his betrayer, Judas, he turned to his disciples and said, "Love like this." This is something the world had never seen before.

New Definition of Worship

With this new kind of love, Jesus turned our definition of worship on its head. He once said that if while offering something to God we remember that we owe something to a brother, we should leave our offering where it is and go be reconciled with that brother. Do you get what he is saying? He is telling us that our relationships with one another *are* worship to God. Caring for one another *is* an offering to God. As Jesus reminded his followers, "I desire mercy, not sacrifice."[13] How hard the Pharisees found it to swallow his words! They would much rather study their laws and attend to their own personal pursuits of holiness than lower themselves to become servants of one another.

I wonder if it is even possible to truly love someone who is separate from yourself. He instructed us to love one another *as ourselves*. In our natural selves, that cannot be done. But what if we were to be made *one* with each other? What if we became members of one another so that what happens to one happens

---

[13] Matthew 9:13, cf. Hosea 6:6

to all? The Lord Jesus made us one with each other just as he and the Father are one with each other.[14] He has thereby formed a Body for himself which will naturally take care of itself, because that's what members of a body do.

I took up running a few years ago because I had gained too much weight. Over several months I conditioned myself to rise at 5:30 in the morning, stretch, and run for about three miles almost every day. It took a lot of willpower and practice to form a habit around making myself out of breath! But eventually it paid off. After several months of running I developed an infection on one of my toes which temporarily railroaded the whole thing. Previously, my whole body had been engaged in daily exercise. Now my whole attention turned to care for this swollen foot which kept me from even walking without difficulty. Why couldn't I disregard something so insignificant as my little toe in the interests of the rest of my body? Because it's all connected. I'm all one organism. When my toe hurts, my whole body devotes its attention toward nursing it back to health. That's the way a body works.

In the Body of Christ, we are one organism, and the problems of one are the problems of all. Do you not find that this is the case in your church? If you don't, perhaps it's because you don't function as a body. Your church may not even know that it is one Body. Unless they are reminded in practical terms, how will they know? If they only interact with one another over coffee and doughnuts for five minutes before Sunday School,

---

[14] John 17:21-23

how can they possibly function like a body? Like I said before, the way we meet has got to change! Or better yet, the way we *live* and *relate to one another* could use an extreme makeover.

Paul's Favorite Metaphor

Despite the attention I have just given to the Church as a Body, did you know that this is not Paul's most common metaphor for the people of God? Nor is it the bride, the temple, the mountain, the city, or the kingdom. The most fundamental image of the Church for Paul is the *family*. His most common reference for the Church sneaks past our notice because of its frequency and familiarity.[15] His favorite name for believers is "brothers and sisters," a term he uses 131 times in his letters.[16]

I think we overlook this word because its significance so rarely finds expression in our relationships with one another. At best, some churches reserve the word "brother" as a title or an epithet for preachers or other staff members. "Brother Fred is going to be speaking tonight on the importance of stewardship, and bringing our tithes and offerings into the storehouse" Rarely do we consider working out in practical terms what it means to be brothers and sisters in Christ. Any way you slice it, we will not grasp the meaning of this new relationship until we are more intimately involved in one another's lives than we already are. For Paul, calling his fellow believers "brothers and

---

[15] Banks, p.50.

[16] Literally the word *adelphoi* includes both genders, so "brothers and sisters" are both included.

sisters" was second nature to him. He saw the Church as a real family.

Jesus himself first proclaimed this radical redefinition of the family after he heard that his mother and brothers were looking for him one day.[17] He responded that from now on his true family would not be determined by blood relations. From that moment on, his true mother and brothers would be those who share in the same spiritual life and calling as he has. Considered against the backdrop of ancient Mediterranean culture, his statement must have carried real shock value to his listeners. For their place and time, blood relations trumped all other social ties. Not so, however, for the community that Jesus came to create. His true family would transcend blood relations. Followers of his would find in one another their true identities, their true context, their true community.

The people I meet with are closer than family to me. The brothers I meet with know me very well. They probably know the kind of things I will say in a situation before I even open my mouth. And I know my sisters, too, their strengths and their weaknesses; and they know mine. I bear the weight of their "life issues" and they shoulder mine as well. When one of us needs something, the rest of us take ownership of that and do what we can to meet each other's needs. We don't always do it well, but we don't stop trying, either. We know who we are to one another. We are brothers and sisters, and we do not take that lightly. We are a family, and we are meant to act as one.

---

[17] Mk.3:34-35

Incidentally, this is one of the main reasons I think believers should meet in homes. Only home meetings capture and express the family atmosphere of the Church.[18] It's hard to see the Church as a family when our meetings only happen in large, formal gatherings in auditoriums with people sitting in pews, looking at the back of each other's heads. The same thing goes for meeting in classrooms with metal chairs, fluorescent lighting, teachers, and roll sheets. It's difficult to get to know one another well in this kind of environment. Formality seems to breed pretense. Well-groomed people in coats and ties (or high heels and hose) are more likely to smile and say everything is "fine," regardless of the state of their lives at the time. But if you put the same people in comfortable, everyday clothes in someone's living room, or kitchen, or back yard, it's a different story entirely. Meeting in homes is how the early Church began, and I think we would do well to return to such simpler, more natural venues.[19]

The Centrality of Love in the New Testament

From time to time I like to print out books of the New Testament so that I can read them more easily. I like to cut and paste chapters from one of the many online Bible websites, then remove all the verse numbers so that the gospel or letter looks

---

[18] See Frank Viola's *Reimagining Church* for a good discussion of this idea (Colorado Springs: David C. Cook, 2008), pp. 83-96.
[19] Merely meeting in a home doesn't achieve the kind of community I am promoting here. It's not about the location. It's about organic authenticity. You can meet in a home and never approach real community.

a little bit more like it was originally written (except in English!). Then I can find a quiet place to sit down and read, say, the letter to the Philippians in its entirety—in one sitting. I recommend doing this sometime yourself. Reading a New Testament letter from beginning to end gives you a feel for its content so much better than bouncing around from verse to verse and from book to book using a topical search or something like that. When I sit down with the letters, I often come with one or two questions in mind: What takes first importance in each letter, and what does Paul or John or Peter (or whoever) give them to *do*? In other words, what matters most to them, and when each of them finally gets around to issuing imperatives, what do they tell them to do?

What strikes me again and again as I do this is the centrality that Paul and John give to believers loving one another. I was initially surprised to find that saving the lost world hardly gets mentioned at all. *Changing the world* never seems to even occur to them. But taking care of our brothers and sisters seeps into nearly every chapter. Whenever they get around to telling us what our main task is, it always lands here. Personal holiness and sanctification seem to be expressed primarily in terms of our interactions with each other. Even worship toward God often gets subsumed under this central activity. Reading the New Testament like this makes it abundantly clear that loving one another in his name is what we are about.

Notice what Paul talks about whenever he reaches the climax of each letter. He always ends up talking about love. Consider when the Corinthians were splitting into opposing groups during meals and creating chaos during meetings. They were having what appeared to be two or three different kinds of meetings at the same time and place. Paul responded to this situation by encouraging them to resolve their differences in the interests of love. Why should they eat all together instead of separately in groups? Because of love. Why should they learn to look past theological differences and peacefully coexist with each other? Because love matters more than knowledge.[20] Why does it matter if everyone in a meeting is speaking in tongues without any interpretations for the ones listening? Because a meeting is not a place for a room full of individuals to each experience their own personal time with God.

We come together to edify and encourage one another. If we cannot understand one another's speech, or if we cannot enter into one another's worship experience and fellowship with God *together*, then we are just making noise.[21] Paul's letter to the Corinthians climaxes with Chapter Thirteen, which has become a classic statement about love (Love is patient, love is kind...). Corinth was a church in love with the gifts of the Spirit. Now they were learning from Paul that taking care of one another matters more than showing off your gifts.

---

[20] Rom.8:1; 13:2
[21] 1 Cor.13:1-2

The letter to the Philippians goes the same way. While this church seemed to show fewer signs of division or immaturity, the heart of his message to them was the same. He gave them a beautiful description of loving one another: "Make my joy complete by being of the same mind, maintaining the same love, united in spirit, intent on one purpose."[22] Like his statements to the Corinthians, his words to the Philippians reveal the centrality of love in the house of God. It is from this chapter that we learn the essence of love: "With humility of mind, regard one another as more important than yourselves." He goes on to show how this very essence was expressed in the incarnation of God in Christ, who took on the form of a servant out of love for his people. A house full of people following this lead would prove the active presence of this great Servant among us. Surely the world would notice something like that!

Each of Paul's letters eventually comes around to this central theme. As the letter to the Romans moves to its conclusion, he gives a very practical description of love in Chapter Twelve: "Love without hypocrisy...be devoted to one another...contributing to the needs of the saints...rejoice with those who rejoice and weep with those who weep." His answer to each of the possible problems that the church in Rome may face is to "pursue the things which make for peace and the building up of one another."[23] Likewise, he encourages the

---

[22] Phil.2:2
[23] Rom.14:19

Thessalonians to "increase and abound in love for one another, and for all people."[24]

That last statement reveals that the love of God is not *exclusive* of the world. His love sends rain on the unjust as well as the just. Often the radical nature of that love becomes more obvious when he shows his care for the well-being of his enemies. However, his love seems to place a priority on caring for the needs of the saints. As he told the Galatians, "while we have opportunity, let us do good to all people, and especially to those who are of the household of faith."[25]

If we cannot learn to care for those within the house of God, then our works of charity and mercy toward the rest of the world seem hollow and pretentious to me. You can give all your possessions to feed the poor and yet still not truly love.[26] *It is easier to be noble toward unbelievers and people you hardly know.* The real test of your love comes when the people with whom you share your life need forgiveness for the thirtieth time. If we can learn to love one another, loving those outside the house of God should be a piece of cake.

Paul is not alone in placing love at the center of the life of the Church. We have already seen how John equated love for our brother with love for God. But Peter also returns again and again to this main exhortation: "Fervently love one another from the heart...Be hospitable to one another without

---

[24] 1 Thess.3:12

[25] Gal.6:10

[26] 1 Cor.13:3

complaint...clothe yourselves with humility toward one another...greet one another with a kiss of love."[27] Similarly, the writer to the Hebrews asks us to "consider how to stimulate one another to love and good deeds."[28] This one characteristic marks us as children of God, and by this the world knows that we are his.

Love in Action

I have seen his love at work among the saints with whom I live. I've watched brothers repair cars, washing machines, computers, roofs, and flooring for sisters who don't have husbands at home to do those kinds of things. I've seen an entire church turn out to help new families move into the neighborhood, even helping them financially so that they can purchase their new home. We've installed air conditioners, painted houses, cut yards, planted gardens, cooked meals, and washed clothes for one another. We've held each other's hands through scary and painful times. We've tended to each other's needs through illness, injuries, births, weddings, strokes, heart attacks, and deaths. I could go on and on.

I could tell you about the time that five or six brothers rushed over to the home of an elderly couple who were out of the country as their home began to flood. We tossed furniture to one another and grabbed lamps, pictures, books, and clothes to take to higher ground even as the flash flood crept up to the

---

[27] 1 Pet.1:22; 4:8-9; 5:5, 14
[28] Heb.10:24

door of their home. I could also tell how several of us met with lawyers, attended meetings, and pestered local councilmen until they agreed to compensate the same elderly couple for their house when it finally did flood.

Then there is the sister who developed medical problems that occasionally prevent her from driving for months at a time. I've seen the church come together to provide her with rides to and from work every day, even though it is out of almost everyone's way. No one ever suggests that they are less than completely willing to do this for her because *that's just who we are to one another.* We are a family. Brothers and sisters do these kinds of things for one another without question. We hardly give it a second thought.

When we lay our lives down for each other, we prove that Christ is risen and living among us today. God has orchestrated all of history toward that very end. Through our love for one another the invisible God becomes visible on the earth again. By looking at us the world can see what the Creator is like. "No one has seen God at any time; [but] if we love one another, God abides in us...By this we know that we abide in him and he is in us, because he has given us of his Spirit."[29] We bear one another's burdens, testifying to our solidarity, our oneness. Jesus said that this will demonstrate to the world that his claims are true.[30] Only the risen and indwelling Christ could

---

[29] 1 Jn.4:12-13
[30] John 17:20-21

make us one. When we treat one another like true brothers and sisters, his presence in the Church becomes undeniable.

A New Light Dawning

Imagine living your whole life in the dark of night, groping your way around and stumbling over every rock and stump. Imagine the mistakes you would learn to accept as normal and the people you would follow simply because they sound like they know more about where they are going than you do. That is the kind of existence that most live, whether they realize it or not. Our "postmodern" culture epitomizes this condition in the way that it embraces uncertainty and confusion. Particularly when it comes to interpersonal relationships, many seem to have given up hope of ever understanding what satisfies the human soul. We have come to accept dysfunction, alienation, and loneliness as simple facts of life. If you don't believe me, simply witness the meandering aimlessness of the relationships in movies like *Lost in Translation* or *Garden State*. More than that, watch the real-life confusion in the personal lives of our wealthiest and most successful celebrities. I don't mean to imply that they are worse off than the rest of us. They simply personify the weaknesses inherent in all of us.

But through his coming kingdom a new light is dawning in our midst. This light comes from him who made us in his own likeness. He knows what we are made of, and he knows what makes us tick. He knows that we are designed for something so much higher than the self-absorption that has gripped us for all these years. This light shines among us when the saints come together in his name to offer up ourselves in the interests of one another. In this light, all the strange deformities of fallen human nature lie exposed like a disease in the daylight. This exposing, yet healing light envelops us as we share Christ with one another.

In this light, the childish ways in which we operate become clear to us. For example, those who do not know the Lord may conceal their business dealings to cover their own dishonesty, but a brother in Christ can not just let that slide. That's not who we are. Unbelievers can mistreat coworkers without the hindrance of a Christ-inhabited conscience. A child of God will never be able to dismiss that from his memory. I'm not saying that Christians don't sin, too. I'm saying that the light of Christ in us will not allow us to sweep what we do under the rug. That's already true to some degree in our individual lives. But when you put a whole community of light-bearers together, the light shines too brightly to ignore.

It is in this light that we learn to be free from our greatest enemy: ourselves. If we walk in the light as he is in the light we have fellowship with one another.[31] That light and that fellowship go together. As I live in the light of the Christ that dwells in my brothers and sisters in the Church, I come to see myself for who I am. I learn to put away those things that are beneath the children of God. In the light of his grace, we are freed from the bondage of corruption and brought into the

---

[31] 1 Jn.1:7

glorious liberty that our fallen minds could hardly imagine. This is salvation to the uttermost. The good news is so much more than we ever thought!

Chapter Ten:

How Do We Get There From Here?

By now you must be asking: All this is great, but how does it come to pass? How do these high and wonderful things become a practical reality? In case you haven't guessed it yet, there's not an easy answer to that question. I cannot give you a five-step program to move a group of people into the eternal purpose of God. The Spirit of God is not mechanical like that. He will not be packaged and sold like the latest exercise equipment. What I *can* give you is an explanation of the things that I have observed which accompany a collective experience of Christ in the church. By no means do I have this thing "figured out." But I can take you to the end of where I have gone in hopes that you may take his testimony higher and farther than I could ever imagine.

It All Starts Here

Have you ever considered that all living things on our planet depend on light? Without light, plants could not live and therefore neither could anything else. Life always begins with light. Our sun is food for everything green. Perhaps that explains why people have worshiped the sun since our most primitive days. Since life begins with light, God first created light. Life in the Spirit is the same way. Spiritual life begins with light. That light comes from the revelation of the person and work of Christ.

Some people get nervous when you say that we need revelation. Reformed theologians in particular have a hang-up about using that word. To them, this term signifies only the most authoritative communication from God. They prefer to reserve this word for canonical literature only (i.e., the Bible itself). If you say there can be more revelation, you're saying we need to add something to our Bibles. But that's not what I'm saying. On the other hand, some preachers are always claiming that they have some "revelation" from God. By this they mean that you should do whatever they say. This kind of talk can show up in a ploy for authority in the church. That's not what I'm talking about, either.

Paul prayed in Ephesians that we might receive a spirit of wisdom and revelation so that "the eyes of our heart" may see what are the riches of the glory of his inheritance in us.[1]

---

[1] Eph. 1:17-18

Whether you call that revelation or "illumination" (somehow that satisfies some theologians), the point is that we can always have a greater insight into who Christ is, and what he has accomplished. Paul could ask for no more important thing than that we may *see better* with the eyes of our hearts the greatness of the One whom we have received. In Christ, God has deposited all the treasures of wisdom and knowledge.[2] He himself is that Tree whose fruit is love, joy, peace, and all the rest. All that we could ever need is deposited *in him*. But we will never own those great things if we do not internally grasp the fullness of who he is.

When Jesus first began to speak about the coming kingdom of God, he told a story about a farmer who sowed some seed. Some of the seed fell on a path and became food for the birds, while the rest of it fell into different kinds of soil. Only the seeds that fell into the good soil bore fruit. Somehow this was like the kingdom of God. He later told his disciples that this seed was the word of God. He went on to explain that the good soil represented those who received the word of God, gripping it tightly. Those who treasure the communication of God will see the kingdom blossom and grow like the lush garden that he intended to plant here in the first place (Notice that the second Adam came to complete the work that the first Adam failed to do).

---

[2] Col.2:3

Thus Saith the Lord

For this reason, the speaking of the word of God will always remain central to the life of the Church. *It need not come only from "preachers," though.* We must see that we all share a common calling to speak the word of God to one another. The righteous live by faith, and faith comes through hearing the word of Christ.[3] But how can we believe in what we have never heard? We need the ministry of the word before we can go anywhere new in Christ. We need God speaking in our midst, and that will take what every member of the Body of Christ can supply.

I must stress that this does not mean merely preaching the Bible. We've had lots of that and little real fruit to show for it. The way we preach the Bible does little to shatter our hardened hearts and our calcified traditions. In fact, the way we approach the Bible seems only to preserve and immortalize whatever we already think and do. Those who bang the loudest on their Bibles, telling us to submit ourselves to the authority of "God's Word," usually mean that we must listen to *them* and accept *their* particular interpretation of whatever is contained inside that book.[4] But the word of God is more dynamic than that. The word of God is living and active, and it cannot be reduced to the pages of a single book. It's like John said at the

---

[3] Rom.10:17

[4] For an excellent discussion about this little "slight of hand," read N.T. Wright's book *The Last Word* (New York: HarperCollins, 2005).

CHRIST IN Y'ALL | 154

end of his gospel—there are more things about Christ to be written than all the books in the world could ever contain.[5]

Do not imagine that God quit speaking the moment the last pages of the Bible were bound. He still speaks today. Tozer put it well:

> To jump from a dead, impersonal world to a dogmatic Bible is too much for most people...A silent God suddenly began to speak in a book and when the book was finished lapsed back into silence again forever. Now we read the book as the record of what God said when he was for a brief time in a speaking mood.[6]

Don't get me wrong—God's words to ancient Israel and to the first-century Church still speak to us today. But God is not yet finished speaking to his people. His *current speaking* is our daily bread. Without his voice sounding in our innermost ears, we are like a ship without wind for our sail, dead in the water.

Looking back through the history of God's people, we discover that the word of God always played a central role in God's activity. Whenever something new and important was about to happen, the story would always begin with "the word of the Lord came to [whomever]." On the other hand, when nothing had happened for ages among them, it would say that "the word of the Lord was rare in those days."[7] They were told to treasure his words and submerge themselves in them by

---

[5] John 21:25
[6] Tozer, p.81.
[7] 1 Sam.3:1

placing them everywhere. They were to place them on the doorway, on their hands, and even on their foreheads. In other words, he wanted them to immerse themselves in—and surround themselves with—his word, because that is where our life comes from. Our bodies may need bread, but our spirits live by every word that proceeds from the mouth of God.[8]

People in the Old Testament loved to say "thus saith the Lord" when they spoke to one another. What nerve they had to claim his authority when they spoke! People like Jeremiah understood that what drove him was the word of God deposited in him, like a fire shut up in his bones.[9] Under those circumstances it just wouldn't do to keep it inside. It was meant to come out so that God's people can be nourished. Lest you think this role was meant only for a special class of prophets, consider the promise that God made through Joel. He declared that one day he would pour out his Spirit on *everyone*. Everyone would prophesy, even down to the "nobodies."[10] That day indeed came when the Church was born. Peter made sure that everyone knew it when it happened.[11] The ministry of the word of God has been given to all of us now, and that is how we will begin to realize the kingdom of God.

---

[8] Deut.8:3
[9] Jer.20:9
[10] Joel 2:28
[11] Acts 2:14ff

Where Does it Come From?

So where do we hear him, and how does he speak? As I look around me and ask myself that question, I find that the word of God comes from three places. First, it comes from our own personal pursuit of God, as we listen for him to speak to us in normal everyday ways. We read books, we read the scriptures, we sing and listen to music. We not only sing to one another, but we also sing when we are alone, reminding ourselves of what we know to be true. Often we appropriate popular tunes and rewrite our own words to them, giving new wings to the words that we have received. Anything and everything can become an opportunity to hear the Spirit of God speak to us. You need only come with a sincere heart that is open to receive whatever he has to say. You can hear him speak in a movie theater, in a grocery checkout line, or on the radio on the way home from work.

There's really no limit to all the ways you can encounter his voice in your daily life. The only thing that this requires is an expectant heart, ready and willing to hear from him. *To the receptive heart, everything becomes a vehicle for the voice of God.* Dreams, music, silence, and even the changing of seasons begin to speak their knowledge of him. Lovingly, relentlessly, he has been coming to you, steadily revealing himself to you all these years. All you really need is the fervent desire to hear him speak.

The second place that we find the voice of God, perhaps the most common way, is in one another. I hear him speak through my brothers and sisters in the church. They open their mouths and the speaking of the Spirit of God becomes daily food for me. The people with whom I meet take seriously Paul's exhortation to "Let the word of Christ richly dwell among you."[12] As Peter said, when we speak to one another, we speak as those speaking the very words of God.[13] We do not take lightly that God has given us the honor of speaking to one another on his behalf. When we speak and listen to one another, we come with an expectation that the Spirit of Christ will inhabit our words and produce in us the life of God.

Incidentally, the group I live and meet with feels free to do this because we have taken the radical step of pursuing God outside the walls of a traditional church environment. Each of us in our own way has discovered that the typical church setting did not provide an opportunity for this kind of free-flowing mutual edification. You can't interrupt the sermon, and you won't get very far away from the Sunday School lesson's prescribed topic before someone redirects everything back to the original plan. In the end, the layman's contribution is valued far less than the minister's. I am convinced that as long as that distinction exists there will be an insurmountable block to the voice of the Lord among his people. If you want to open the floodgates of the River of Life, you will have to provide a way for the people of God to speak.

When my church group assembles, we speak to one

---

[12] Col.3:16
[13] 1 Pet.4:11

another out of our own daily experiences with the Lord. Sometimes this comes from meeting alone with God, and sometimes with a partner or two. We sometimes meet early in the morning before work, or else whenever we get a moment free in the evening. We can get together easily because we all intentionally live very close to one another. Most of us bought houses on the same two or three connected streets. Because of our physical proximity to one another, we often bump into each other and spend time together on the spur of the moment. A group of people living as a community can accomplish things like that. Although this kind of lifestyle cuts against the grain of American "cocooning," we have come to see it as an indispensable factor in our spiritual lives.

The third place that we look for God to speak to us is in those gifted individuals who enable us to make the most out of those first two channels of spiritual life. God has given these people to the church in order for the Body of Christ to mature and grow up into Christ, our Head. In Ephesians, Paul lists four of these kinds of people (although I don't see why we should read that as an exhaustive list). He mentions apostles, prophets, evangelists, and pastors/teachers. God gives each of these to the Church to enable the rest of the Body to function according to each member's various gifting. Their job is to help the rest of us function without necessarily becoming *dependent upon them* for everything.

Where I live, we call that "overfunctioning." When someone within a fellowship overfunctions, it stifles the healthy development of the other members of the Body. I will not attempt here to go into a prolonged explanation of these gifts. If you'd like to read a detailed discussion about this I would recommend that you read either *The Normal Christian Church Life* by Watchman Nee, or else *Reimagining Church* by Frank Viola.[14]

Organic Leadership

Because of the funny way that we approach the Bible, any list of gifts like the one in Ephesians 4 gets terribly misused by well-meaning people. They read that these roles exist in the Church and conclude that exactly these four gifts (or five, depending on their translation of the pastor/teacher pairing) should *always* be in *every* church. They make it a rule and try to squeeze all churches into the same mold. But Paul's point in this passage was not to draw our attention to mechanics or methodology. His point was that God provides members of the Body of Christ who can help the rest of the saints move further on into the deep things of Christ. Some call these "equippers." According to Ephesians 4, God empowers them to enable others so that the Church can mature *unto the measure of the fullness of Christ*. That's an exciting prospect! Something as glorious as that must look at least a little bit different from place to place and from group to group. Unfortunately, not everybody appreciates diversity.

---

[14] Watchman Nee, *The Normal Christian Church Life* (Anaheim: Living Stream, 1980); Frank Viola, *Reimagining Church* (Colorado Springs: David C. Cook, 2008).

Why must we be so rigid about our expectations for the way things are supposed to happen? The religious nature of the flesh always drives us to extremes. Most churches read Paul's list of gifts to the Church and conclude that it is an exhaustive list. Every church must conform, or else they are illegitimate. Rather than allowing these functions (or something like them) to naturally appear and develop over time, they believe you must begin with all four (or five) ministries already present and in full force. Church leaders see it as their duty to make these functions appear. This eventually smothers the organic growth of the church. In the end I believe it's not important *what you call* the various functions and gifts within the Body of Christ. What matters is that they should exist without being forced upon a group. The group should discover the specifics on their own, provided that they get a little help from folks who have a clue about the deeper things of Christ.

On the other hand, many other groups try to run the opposite direction. They resolve to resist and suppress the development of these kinds of functions almost entirely. Perhaps they got burned at some point, and they fear that their new group will too easily become as dead and ritualistic as the kind of church they just left. House churches fall into this opposite ditch after discovering the beauty of having every member function without special leaders dominating the church. They want to avoid the domineering pastor/elder tradition that we've inherited from centuries of Christian history, so *they resist leadership of any kind*. Can you see how this will eventually stunt the growth of the church and keep her in an indefinite state of infancy? A healthy, growing church will experience elements of leadership along the way to maturity. Some can learn to lead without taking over.

Many of these "gifted ones" that God gives to the church provide different forms of the ministry of the word. The Church lives by the speaking of God in her midst; so he nourishes her by providing exactly what she needs when she needs it. Somehow we must learn to allow these functions to develop "organically"—naturally—according to God's plan for each individual church, without trying to squeeze all churches into the same frame. After a church has been planted, they must be allowed to develop according to their individual differences as God provides through the functioning of each member.

GETTING STARTED

A good way to start down this road is to pass around books or websites that give a flavor of what you're after. If others like what they read or hear, then maybe you've got the start of something there. Maybe you could visit some groups that are already pursuing deeper things to see if they have any pointers to offer you. Do a little research online[15] and maybe

---

[15] For some suggestions, see the list of websites included at the end of this book.

take a trip or two with another believer with whom you can discuss what you find.

If you are already a part of a group that is trying out new things, you can always begin with meals in each other's homes. It's a great way to get to know one another. You're less likely to be overly religious or artificial while chewing food in front of other people. Talk, laugh, and eat together while getting to know each other's stories. Maybe after a few months of that you can begin to think about things like singing together, praying together, or seeking out some kind of ministry. But we all need a little bit of time to "detox." We've got years of habits and thought patterns to break free from, so give it time. Don't be in too much of a hurry. Think in terms of years, not days.

One challenge you will face is that almost everyone has preconceived notions about what a church should look like and act like. Almost everyone has been affected at some level by the church, for better or for worse. Even those who have hardly ever set foot inside a church building have a father or grandfather who was probably a deacon or an elder, and was there every time the doors were opened. Any church planted in this country will therefore have people with varying amounts of experience with the Lord. Some may have been Christians all their lives, while others will hardly know him at all.

This kind of variation will require a good deal of patience on the part of everyone involved. Some will have a lot to learn, while others will have a lot of *unlearning* to do. In this environment, believers who have known God their entire lives will suddenly find that there are sides to him they have never seen. It will take an adventurous spirit to reach for the highest and best that God can bring to the saints. It will also take humility and a willingness to be led for a time by those who have had more experience in this open participatory kind of church experience. In other words, churches have the greatest hope for survival when they are helped by people who have done this before.

Some believers will decide, as we did, to live in close proximity to one another. When that happens, problems multiply like rabbits! I am convinced that churches like ours need someone who is not "a part of the problem" to offer third-party guidance from time to time. Many groups begin spontaneously and don't believe that they need anyone to help them "find their legs." But groups that receive some kind of outside help fare much better. They have a much better chance of living beyond their third or fourth year of existence. Those churches that Paul planted needed ministry from him (and others) years after their genesis. In fact, their many problems are the reason we have half of our New Testament in the first place! We should expect at least as many challenges among the groups that start today.

Most importantly, those who help a church get going must start them off with a high vision and deep insight into the person and work of Christ. Remember that the Church lives on the revelation of Christ. *The roots of the Church will only be as deep as the gospel that it receives.* Therefore the first order of business is for those who minister to provide as much insight into the mystery of Christ as they have. Those who minister to the church, especially those who have been called to start churches, serve as "stewards of the mystery."[16] It is their job to both preach the gospel to those who don't know the Lord and to expose believers to the deep things of Christ. Whether this ministry comes from the outside or from within the group, believers should seek after those who truly know the Lord well. Those who lead must know how to endure the cross, laying down their own desires and ambitions for the sake of those to whom they minister.

It can be hard to find people like that. It can be especially hard to find individuals who fit this bill and don't have a strong personal need to control a group. People who know they have a higher vision than those around them easily fall under the delusion that they always know what's best for a church. But our way of life is not an exact science. What works for one group may not fit another group at all. The Spirit will have to guide us every step of the way.

We Need One Another

Those who minister to the Church must know real humility. There is a give and take—a kind of mutual submission—in the relationship between churches and those who serve them. Neither party needs to entertain the idea that they alone know the mind of the Lord at any given moment. We

---

[16] Eph. 3:2-12

are on this journey together and we should expect to make a lot of mistakes along the way. The important thing is that we follow the example of the One who is always laying down his life for those whom he loves. We are not out to preserve our lives but to lose them. If we can remember that, we can go anywhere.

We must also remember that the goal is for the whole Body to learn how to function according to what each part and joint can supply.[17] We are reassembling Christ when we come together, and it will take the whole Church to express the fullness of who he is. In terms of the local church this means that *the group must not become passive recipients of the ministry of only one or two individuals*. It will not do to have one giant mouth or one giant tongue surrounded by a room full of ears. The whole Body needs to learn how to function in interdependence between all the members of the fellowship. So whether we're talking about the church planter coming in from the outside or an elder-type ministering from within, the test of that ministry will be in whether or not the rest of the saints learn to function without their constant supervision.

Let us also acknowledge that it takes *all* the saints to express who he is, not merely the members of our own group. He has called his own from among people in every century and every nation. He has captured different elements of his own nature at different times and in different groups. One group does a good job of expressing his power while another group

---

[17] Eph. 4:16

expresses his forgiveness. Another group has discovered his wisdom and knowledge while yet another excels in his love. We should relate ourselves to the larger Body of Christ with a sincere spirit of humility, realizing that no one group can ever claim to "have it all." We can learn from one another and should not be afraid to interact with saints from groups who "do it differently" from us. Openness to the larger Body of Christ is a sign of health in a church.

I believe it is also important to maintain a willingness to try new things. No one has this whole thing figured out (not even the people who write books about it!). We will need an attitude of experimentation in all that we do. Just because something brought life to the church years ago doesn't mean that it should be bronzed and installed permanently in the way we do things. The way we meet should change from time to time. The songs we sing should adapt and grow to express each new thing that a church discovers. Even the vocabulary we use should change over time to reflect the lessons that we've learned along the way. Growth and change are necessary to all living things, so they are signs of health as well.

A Word of Warning

Let's start by admitting that we don't live in the first century. In our quest to emulate the New Testament Church, we should take care not to fall into the trap of trying to copy everything that they did. There are too many things that distinguish our time from theirs. Travel, technology, language, education, and perhaps especially our political and religious environments are vastly different today from how things were in the first-century Roman Empire. We sometimes compare apples and oranges when we ask, "How did they do it in the early Church?" Rob Bell insightfully argued in *Velvet Elvis* that we have to get creative in our approach because the practice of our faith is more of an art form than a mechanical science. The times in which we live will keep changing, and the Church will have to adapt and find new ways to express who Christ is to the world.

One of the stickiest questions we must ask ourselves is: How do we relate to all the institutional churches that already exist in our day? The first century believers had to figure out their relationship to the Jewish faith. We will find ourselves wondering how to get along with the rest of the Christian faith! More often than not, you will find that believers who are used to congregational church models will not be receptive to your new ideas. Christians who want to experiment with "deeper things" and new ways of meeting will have to look elsewhere to find a group of believers with whom they may embark on this adventure. They may find it easier to try to win some unbelievers to the Lord instead.

I believe most folks who have tried this way of life would agree that real "body life" needs an environment with more freedom than can be found in a brick-and-mortar kind of church. Trying to inject this into a traditional church setting will only upset the leadership structures already in place. Springing "open meetings" on a minister who takes complete responsibility for everything is unrealistic.

Those in leadership continue to believe that it is their God-given responsibility to maintain and preserve the institutional form of their church, no matter what. Think of all the labor that went into raising the funds for the building itself. Think of all the furniture, the stained-glass windows, the activities building and the educational space. Think about the salaries of the staff members who depend on the tithes and offerings for their livelihood. These things are set in place and will not go away by simply changing our theology.

The Problem of Wineskins

It took me a while to admit that "body life" cannot survive long within the traditional church setting because these two things are antagonistic to each other. Jesus said that no one pours new wine into old wineskins. They will pop and all the wine will be lost—both the new and the old. Like oil and water, vibrant "church life" and traditional church will not coexist for long in the same place, because they operate on totally different principles. Traditional church practices are based on the repetition of methods and programs. They are rooted in structures of static, official leadership. Dynamic "body life" cannot be contained within such an immovable environment, and it will always stretch such structures beyond their capacity to contain it.

If you try to introduce Spirit-led community life into a place where there is already a leader or group of leaders guiding the group, you will force the current leaders to forfeit their function and positions (which they believe were assigned to them by God). No sensible builder would build something new on top of existing structures; he will look for a clearing—an open place with no obstacles. That's why Paul asserted that he would never do something so foolish as to try to build the Church of God on top of someone else's already-laid foundation.[18] Do not bother trying to "stay within the system," hoping to reform it or inject life into it. You're just going to make a mess.

A brief note about church staff members: When they are resourceful, observant people, you will ask yourself: "If this is such an obvious problem, why have they not seen it and addressed it?" But look closer and you will see that staff members are already experiencing a level of "body life" because *they are allowed to function!* They see each other daily (community), they plan and guide the direction of the church, and they even get to open their mouths in the meetings! The problem here is not that a few specially marked individuals get to do this, but that the rest of us don't! We should all be "staff members" from now on. No distinctions. The next time your pastor declares that "every member is a minister," you should ask him which Sunday you will get to preach and pick the songs!

---

[18] Rom. 15:20

Of course, I would love for some church to prove me wrong! In my crazier moments I dream that a church staff or a congregation may one day ask for help in transitioning from a clergy-centered model to a more lay-centered, home-based model. Perhaps some waning congregational church may one day decide to start meeting in homes, turning their building into something more useful on a daily basis, like a homeless shelter with a built-in soup kitchen. All those cushioned pews could sleep a lot of folks, not to mention all those classrooms that sit vacant 99% of the week! They even could still use the worship center from time to time when they want to assemble all in the same place. The staff could continue serving the needs of those who need help the most. Some of them could even elect to learn a profitable trade in order to ease the financial burden on the congregation. Many older churches subsist on foundations established by people who died a long time ago. Eliminating the overhead of a full-time staff could free up quite a bit of church funds for things like clothes and food for those who need it most. The possibilities are endless! But then, like I said, these are the dreams that I have in my crazier moments.

Back here in the real world, those of us looking for something different will face some hard questions. Are we willing to cut a path for something new, despite the opposition we will certainly face from those who don't understand what we are doing? We must count the cost and decide if we are up to swallowing the condescension and criticism that friends and family may throw our way as we leave the beaten path. It can be a daunting task to maintain a good relationship with those who "stay in the system," particularly when they believe you are leaving the faith once delivered to the saints. My wife and I have been fortunate in that our families have never given us a hard time about what we are doing. But some will not be so lucky. If we decide to leave, let us resolve to leave with grace and tact, remembering that no one should go where they do not feel led by God's Spirit. And please remember that God's purposes are always larger than the limits of your own vision. He certainly does things within the "stay-inners" that he could never accomplish though the "come-outers."

Down with "Cocooning"

If you get very far down this road, at some point you'll have to address the issue of where you live. I believe that some kind of rearranging of our lifestyles is necessary before we will see much progress toward expressing the coming kingdom of God. I bought a house two doors down from another family in the church for this very reason. Now three other families live within a few houses from the both of us. I sought and found a job within a short drive from our neighborhood so that I wouldn't spend half my day commuting to and from work. I admit that this kind of luck won't be available to everyone, but it's something to consider. I was willing to sacrifice a lot because I found a group of people as hungry as I am to find and experience the Lord in daily life. Sometimes they're a little nutty, but I'll take a bad day among these people over a thousand good days anywhere else!

If a group of people is considering something as radical as moving close to one another, they themselves will also run into this question of location. House churches in the U.S. tend to begin in suburbia, among middle-class, college-educated people. This brings a tendency toward homogenization, which I see as a problem for the long-term growth of these churches. Perhaps it would be better if some adventurous folks would be willing to relocate to more centrally-located urban areas. People there live closer to one another and naturally rub elbows with a wider variety of people. Of course, this brings its own challenges, such as low-performing schools or overpriced housing and/or crime. But these things will not forestall those who feel truly called to this kind of life. Those who follow Jesus Christ have to be a little crazy sometimes! It comes with the territory.

The bottom line is this: We're going to have to be willing to venture out and experiment with the practical expression of the Church. House church isn't the only way to go (although to my mind it's got some key elements that I'd hate to lose). Neither the urban church nor the suburban church can claim exclusively that it is "the way church ought to be." I don't think there is only one way to be the Church. What I do know is that the Church should exist on this earth in real, tangible communities. We must retire the old notion that little pockets of friendship here and there are all we're going to get. I'm pretty sure that's not what Jesus had in mind when he announced that he was going to build his Church. Let us never quit reaching toward the goal of our calling.

Every group needs ministry, and the ministry they receive should be high and choc-full of the centrality and supremacy of Jesus Christ. Their first need will not be to understand what they are supposed to believe about eschatology, or Arminianism vs. Calvinism, or church discipline. Their fundamental need will be to grasp the Lord Jesus as the supply for their every need, both as individuals and as a church. When that fellowship gets on its way, they must first learn how to find the Lord as daily food and drink for their spirits.[19] They will also learn to live as brothers and sisters who love and care for one another in real and practical ways. If they can do those two things, I don't really think it matters *how* they meet, *where* they live, or *when* they gather. The important thing is that they learn to find Christ as their *all*, and that they learn to express that in ways that can be seen and heard and touched. That is what God is after.

---

[19] For more about the Lord as our food and drink, I recommend Mike Morrell's upcoming book *Eat God.*

Chapter Eleven:
Church in a Changing World

‎=====================

Folks who try to do church in the 21ˢᵗ century find that things have been changing lately. At first it's hard to say exactly *what* is changing. Something fundamental has shifted in the world around us and things are not as they once were. We feel these changes in education, in art, in literature, in movies, and even in our homes and our churches. For one thing, people don't respond to the gospel the way they once did. It's almost as if they don't even have a place to put it once they hear it. We have already considered what was wrong with the funny way we tried to share the gospel in the past. Put that together with the way we do church and our faith starts to look less and less relevant to the world around us. Something basic has changed in the world, and the people whose job it is to label these things have given our new condition a name: "Postmodernity."

The term "postmodern" means that much of our culture has left behind the assumptions of the modern era. Older folks remember a time when our value system was clear-cut and deeply ingrained. We were once confident that advances in technology would solve all our problems. Modernity signaled the celebration of rationalism, logic, and systematization. Whether you looked at architecture, landscaping, music, art, or business, you found symmetry and uniformity. Today you are more likely to see diversity, asymmetry, anti-intellectualism, and a celebration of everything in life that's organic, even messy.

Basic social structures like the family have changed, too. They no longer look like they once did, with two happily married parents, three basically disciplined kids, and a dog in the back yard. Today divorced, unmarried, and remarried adults outnumber those who have known only one spouse. Kids today grow up in blended families of every stripe and background you can imagine. People now prefer to live together first, then decide whether or not to get married.

Most alarmingly to some, our evangelical churches have been steadily leaking membership for decades until the only churches left with any kind of growth are the handful of megachurches that can afford the bells and whistles it takes to hold everyone's attention. Barna estimates that as many as 20 million Americans have left the traditional church environment in search of something that better fits their values and internal sense of calling.[1] Many will experiment with house churches, coffee-house ministries, or support groups. Others will gravitate toward the myriad of online "virtual communities," or else quit looking for "church" altogether. Why is all of this happening, and what should be our response to it all?

How Postmodernity Came to Be

Intellectuals tend to blame the rise of postmodernism on the collapse of western philosophy. That story goes something like this: Some time before the Europeans settled in the New World, the intellectual seeds were sown which would later enthrone science over faith in a period we now call the Enlightenment. Philosophers began to separate sense experience from faith and philosophy in a way that made the former look a lot more reliable than the latter. People began to trust the sciences as our answer to all the needs of humanity. But somehow it never occurred to them that *sense experience alone* cannot answer the bigger questions of life, like "Who are we? Why are we here? and Is there a world beyond what our senses can perceive?" Before long many began to doubt whether the big questions could even be answered at all. Science could handle the physical stuff, and anything beyond that became fodder for fairy tales and mythology.

---

[1] http://www.barna.org/FlexPage.aspx?Page=BarnaUpdate&BarnaUpdate ID=241

But by the early 20th century science itself began to tarnish. The deeper we peered into the make-up of the universe the more convinced we became that we don't know what we're talking about. Uncertainty replaced certainty in our study of things both big and small. Then we learned how to split the atom without ever stopping to ask if we really *should*. Our bag of philosophical tools no longer had a way to address issues like that. Two world wars effectively buried the great hope we once had in the myth of progress.

Finally, by the middle of the 20th century, the most influential professors and writers exerted their energy to argue that knowledge itself is impossible, and that truth as we have always conceived of it does not even exist. It was only a matter of time before these beliefs filtered down through art, literature, and film into popular consciousness.[2] Now cynicism and despair permeate our music, our poetry, our movies, and sometimes even our casual conversation.

But there are other factors making this happen as well. I suspect that the way we think has always been greatly influenced by *what we invent*. After someone invented a watch, people began to imagine that the universe runs like a watch. They imagined that the Creator designed the universe so that he could wind it up once and run on its own without his

---

[2] There's a lot more to say about what Postmodernism is and how it came to be, but I'm going to resist the temptation to turn this chapter into a course in philosophy. Instead, I can recommend that interested readers look for books like *Postmodern Times* by Gene E. Veith (Wheaton: Crossway Books, 1994), and *A Primer on Postmodernism* by Stanley Grenz (Grand Rapids: Eerdmans, 1996).

intervention. The printing press changed the way we accessed information and allowed people (other than priests) to publicly share what they were thinking. The industrial revolution reoriented European and American life, starting a relentless movement toward urbanization which continues to affect our lifestyles even today. The telegraph and the telephone connected continents and shortened geographical distances. The electric generator and the light bulb helped us to overcome days and seasons, making us forget about natural cycles and rhythms in life.

The automobile alone has restructured American society in ways that can scarcely be overstated. Once Henry Ford appeared on the scene, dating replaced courtship. Now you could drive far away from each of your homes and your parents would no longer be around to chaperone. These days when you go away to college your significant other will likely not be from your home town, so your parents can no longer really know his or her parents before you've made your selection for life. You'll probably settle down somewhere far away from your parents or else your job will eventually require you to relocate. Most folks no longer live anywhere near the place their parents called home. Our sense of identity and our concept of the family has consequently changed, and we are still dealing with the results.

The airplane, the television, the computer, and now the internet have linked together opposite sides of the planet. Now countries and cultures are blending and interacting in ways they never could before. Perhaps this globalization of our consciousness is responsible for the disorientation and confusion that many feel. There's just too much information to take in! It's too much for most people to sort through. The information overload makes each generation progressively more "A.D.D.," and all the noise and busy-ness becomes a numbing background to our constantly shifting lives.

Looking for Truth

It's no wonder that news channels and high-powered news anchors became such a hot commodity toward the end of the last century. We are desperate for someone to make sense out of all the frantic activity that we see spinning around us. Just tell us what it all means and how we should feel about it! We no longer have our communities of origin – our hometowns and our tightly-knit extended families.[3] They always helped us process and evaluate the things happening around us. That is why chat rooms, blogs, and networking sites like Facebook have become so wildly popular. Online communities give us a sense of belonging to a group, even if it is purely digital. It's better than nothing. We need them because we draw our identity from the community to which we belong.

Even still, we are left wondering how much of what we see and hear is truly real. A generation raised on television and special effects begins to doubt that anything they see is real. You can "photoshop" a picture to look like anything you want.

---

[3] Cf. Mary Pipher, *The Shelter of Each Other* (New York: Random House, 1996), chp.3.

And how do you know if the person you've been emailing really is who he says he is? First our professors told us that we can't know anything for sure. Then our television sets began beaming illusory images into our living rooms every night. Now our online communities are populated with individuals who pretend to be something that they're not. You can see why the postmodern condition is characterized by distrust and uncertainty.

So how does the gospel speak to this situation, and what does the Church in the postmodern world look like? To be honest, these questions are pretty big, perhaps too big for me to get my little brain around. I don't suffer from the delusion that I can see far enough into the future to understand what the Lord (or the world) will do next. But contrary to the postmodern ethos of doubting absolutely everything, I do see a handful of things about the gospel and the Church that I believe give answer to the illnesses that afflict our generation.

Babies and Bathwater

A good starting point would be to acknowledge the places where postmodernism gets it right. For example, when our culture expresses distrust toward people with power, they have good reason for that. After two world wars and two or three more localized wars against communist governments and radical Islamic dictatorships, Americans are losing faith in the inherent goodness of governments (including their own). It is not always easy to evaluate the motives of people in power.

Even the political decisions that seem basically right are not always made for the right reasons. Such is the nature of fallen humanity. But this should not shock followers of the man who said "My kingdom is not of this world." No matter how thankful we are for the religious liberties that a democratic nation affords us, our churches should never equate patriotism with faithfulness to Christ. Jesus instructed us to render unto Caesar that which is Caesar's; but our hearts and our passions will not allow for more than one master at a time.

Likewise postmoderns are right when they criticize so many churches for being out of touch and irrelevant. Traditions which spoke to an earlier generation no longer carry the same significance for people who are my age or younger. The style of music, the clothes, the vocabulary, and the rituals may be precious to the ones who have done church that way their entire lives. But these look totally foreign and unnatural to this newer generation. King James English might as well be words from outer space in our day. I'm not saying that the solution is found in merely mimicking the younger generation's hairstyles, clothes, and vocabulary. What I am saying is that we should be willing to reconsider how much of what we do *has to be done* the way we do it. We must ask hard questions about what is truly sacred and what is merely a human tradition.

Must we meet in a special building with a steeple on top of it? Would you consider us a real church if we didn't? Must there be a traditional church staff, with seminary degrees and regular salaries? Could you consider a group legitimate if it did not employ anyone like that? Must our Eucharist/Lord's Supper be done precisely as it is, or could it be changed up a bit to regain some of the meaning that it has lost? Is Sunday School indispensable? Is it sacrosanct? Did God himself institute dressing up for church? Must we study the Bible by cutting and pasting verses from one book to another according to different topics? Couldn't we rediscover what it's like to know *the story* behind the words? Reworking the way we do these things from time to time would go a long way toward keeping our faith fresh and authentic. We must not hold as sacred anything which has merely come to us as a man-made tradition.[4] That's what got the Pharisees in trouble with Jesus.

Finally, postmoderns rightfully criticize their evangelical predecessors for absorbing the materialism and consumerism of modern society. Witness how the megachurch model follows the modern corporation. Always in search of the next popular trend, they multiply programs and services until they get the desired number of nickels and noses. Folks come, not to give, but to *get*. That's consumerism. And rarely will this kind of church challenge the financial well-being of its members when the poorer members of the church are in need. But you can be sure that the next program that the church has to offer will come complete with a slick brochure and an accompanying t-shirt. That's our materialism.

---

[4] For the most detailed (and footnoted!) study of evangelical church traditions to date, I recommend you read *Pagan Christianity* by Barna and Viola.

The Spirit of the Age

Our overconfidence in our traditions reflects the overconfidence which has characterized modern man since the dawning of the Age of Reason. Stanley Grenz pointed out that the Enlightenment project itself was rooted in the quest to overcome our own limitations through the tireless and methodical use of science and reason. While the Christian faith should have known better, the theology which grew out of this time period adopted the same arrogance that characterized science and philosophy through the Enlightenment years. Quite the opposite, Paul could speak of a basic distrust in human reason as the ultimate measure of truth.[5] Contrast that with the 19th century theologians who learned to view the Bible as a collection of scientific data to be analyzed and classified according to its constituent parts and verses.[6] They reorganized the biblical "data" into an air-tight system of thought and belief until it sparkled like a golden calf.

The careful student of Christian history will recognize in this mentality the early roots of fundamentalism. Treating the Bible like this produced a feeling of absolute certainty toward our own theological framework. Eventually we began to trust the framework itself instead of the truth that it was created to uphold. Over time Christians began to confuse their *thoughts about* God's revelation with the revelation itself. People learned

---

[5] 1 Cor.1:20-21; 2:14-16

[6] A perfect example of this appears in Charles Hodge's *Systematic Theology* (Grand Rapids: Eerdmans, 1968), p.10-11.

to bang their fists on their Bibles and shout something unoriginal about being "faithful to the Word of God." What they didn't realize was that their theology had replaced Christ himself as their ultimate object of devotion. Over time, the unexamined assumptions of so many churches have made them look pitiful and silly to those on the outside. People who grew up in evangelical homes became disillusioned with the pat answers they were given as children. Now many of them have left their faith behind.

We can argue till we're blue in the face about the inerrancy of the scriptures. But it is our *use* of the scriptures that keeps getting us into trouble. We of all people should know that knowledge is not free from human bias. We should not have been caught off guard by the postmodern realization of that fact. Perhaps postmodernism will sound the death knell for the more mindless varieties of fundamentalism, with their worn-out clichés and funny hairdos. In fact, we could all use a healthy dose of epistemological humility.

An Opportune Moment

This moment in history provides us with an excellent opportunity to regain something lost in former generations. After centuries of increasing individualism, our culture has come full circle to the point of rediscovering the value of *community*. In order to keep from drowning in the vast sea of relativism and subjectivity, the postmodern thinker has learned to appreciate the ability that communities have to provide us with a sense of meaning. He knows that communities give us a narrative by which we may evaluate our lives. For the first time in a very long time, the relentless march toward individualism has begun to show signs of turning. People today are reconsidering the necessity of life together with others. Even our city planners and developers have begun to respond to a call for more tightly-knit, walkable communities that counteract the effects of cocooning and suburban sprawl.

Perhaps that is why house churches and cell groups have seen such a resurgence even among traditional Christian churches. Besides finding this environment to be a more comfortable and natural setting for building relationships, believers today are beginning to see the collective nature of the Christian life (hence the title of this book). Traditionally, we have taught spiritual formation as an on-your-own endeavor, or perhaps with one other person (as in the discipleship model). Now some are beginning to crave the interaction of the whole Body of Christ, longing to see him move and act in each and every believer. Taking our cue from the plural pronoun in Galatians 4:19, we are learning that "Christ formed in y'all" takes a whole community to act out.[7]

It will take just such a community to earn the right to speak to a generation overloaded with words and information.

---

[7] Even biblical scholars are adjusting their hermeneutic to account for the more social aspects of the gospel. In my opinion, many of them take this too far, making the social aspects the only meaningful aspects of the work of God in the world and in his people. But this shift in academia demonstrates the sea change occurring in every area of our culture.

Like the people whom Paul encountered in Athens, many today spend the better part of their lives listening to one new thing after another until they forget what it looks like to encounter real truth – truth with teeth. They may have little patience for our *Four Spiritual Laws* or our *Romans Road to Salvation,* but they will not easily dismiss a living community of people rising above their own interests in order to care for one another as a loving family does. Imagine people from different races, different cultures, and different socio-economic strata coming together as one and functioning as a single living organism. You can bet that the world will sit up and take notice of something like that. Jesus said that our learning to live and act as one is the greatest proof to the world that his claims are true.[8]

They Will Know...By Our Love

Thus we have found one answer to our question. How does the gospel speak to the postmodern pessimism toward finding truth and reality? *When the Church becomes an object lesson in transcendence,* we prove Jesus' exclusive claims to ultimate reality. When our lives are governed by his Spirit, we demonstrate that there is in fact a design to life, a way that human nature works. Our increasing freedom from the "tyranny of self" emits an aroma that draws those who hunger and thirst for a righteousness that is real. When the Church becomes a place of grace, a place of mercy, a place for justice, and a house of love, the light of our good news will burn

[8] John 17:20-23

through the fog of postmodern doubt and disillusionment. The sons of Adam and the daughters of Eve will sense their destiny when they encounter it, like so many prodigals finally returning home.

This all works because his sheep know his voice when they hear it. We have come to accept as normal the chaotic noise of so many competing voices. So many rivaling stories each claim the right to be believed. But as the old song says, "We've a story to tell to the nations/That shall turn their hearts to the right." Unlike other stories clamoring for credibility, *our story happens to be true.* We know that it's true because our lives resonate with its message. Our experience bears witness to the truth of the gospel, and its effect on our lives cannot easily be denied.

Postmodern people may have given up hope for ever finding such a thing as a true story. Through the Church, however, their spirits can recognize their origins with or without the assistance of a satisfied mind. They will not be able to deny having encountered the risen Christ in real experience, no matter what their worldview tells them about the inaccessibility of truth. This risen Christ can be found in the hearts of his people, doing what he has always done: giving himself for the sake of another.

It seems no coincidence to me that postmodern thought has leveled its harshest blow to our trust in the meaningfulness of language itself. The God who speaks created us to enjoy language as a sign of our unique place in the order of creation.

Perhaps our language is a means for exercising our authority over creation. Like the story of the tower of Babel, our hope for salvation easily comes to rest on ourselves and our achievements. Then our sovereign God sees fit to dismantle the very thing that enables us to rise above all other creatures – our language. In mercy he comes to disable the arrogant self-confidence of mankind so that we will be ready to receive what he has to say to us. Through all of this, he prepares his people to hear the message of the gospel, which according to Paul carries with it the power to rescue us from the things that enslave us.[9] We speak his words to one another and we are changed.

The practical outworking of the kingdom of God will vary from group to group. We should never tolerate in ourselves the arrogance which asserts that we alone understand what "the true Church" looks like. In reality there must be infinite variety to God's self-expression. But I believe that there are certain aspects of our culture which should not be absorbed by the Church, and I am willing to risk sounding narrow-minded in order to spell out what I think the Church should avoid along the way.

Christ vs. Culture

Obviously the first thing that should not be accepted wholesale by the Church is the all-consuming cynicism and doubt that I've already addressed. A healthy dose of intellectual

[9] Rom.1:16

humility is a good thing; but we need not follow the world into the despair of complete uncertainty. I like a "hermeneutic of suspicion" as much as the next guy. But there are some things that we really *can* know. Our lives can serve as a practical testing ground for the things that we say we believe. Incidentally, if you'd like to read a great book that strikes this balance between humility and despair, I'd recommend that you get a copy of *The Myth of Certainty* by Daniel Taylor. It's a book that will make a lot of sense to the analytical believer who prefers not to check his brain at the door of his faith.

Another facet of postmodern culture which we should approach with some reservation is its obsession with *virtual community*. In case you don't know what I'm talking about, I'll try to explain. I've already mentioned how George Barna has discovered among contemporary evangelicals a seismic shift away from traditional forms of church into alternative modes of expressing the Christian faith.[10] At first glance, that may sound like the kind of movement which a book like this one would encourage. To be sure, many of those millions which Barna has followed are moving into various kinds of experimental home fellowships or other such communities.

But many are not really pursuing real fellowships at all. Some have given up on ever seeing "a real church." They have decided to try following Christ in their own personal way without expecting any kind of community of believers to walk

---

[10] You can read why he calls these people "revolutionaries" in *Revolution*, or you can visit his site: www.barna.org for more information.

beside them in the process. Either they intend to "make the world a better place" through one-on-one relationships with one or two people at a time, or else they are gravitating toward the many networks of individuals who are finding one another by way of the internet. These are what you call "virtual communities."

This phenomenon is simultaneously a blessing and a curse. It is a blessing for those who have no other meaningful contact with people with whom they may truly connect. Folks hungry for something more than what they find in their geographical area cannot be blamed for spending hours in front of their computer screens, combing the web for signs of life. No doubt this new tool presents an amazing opportunity for the spread of the gospel. It creates opportunities for believers to find one another so that they can hook up with each other and pursue the Lord together. The problem comes when the virtual community becomes a substitute for real church.

Many would argue that virtual communities are no less "church" than a group of people occupying the same physical space. They would insist that our definition of community must not be so narrow as to exclude this new and exciting way to fellowship with other believers. But I would have to say that this new kind of "community" leaves out a few key elements of true community which I think cannot be lost.

A virtual community cannot greet one another with a holy kiss. Of course, I don't believe the kiss is the important thing here. What matters is the ability to *see* one another, *touch* one another, and *hold* one another when the need arises. We are physical beings as well as spiritual ones, and we need to be with real people – in the flesh, so to speak. Any who have moved away from their parents can attest to their need to *see* us once in a while. I know my parents would love for me to move my growing family back to their area so that they could watch the kids mature and develop into the young ladies they are becoming. They will never be totally satisfied with emailed pictures or phone calls. They know as well as I that *we need to be near one another.* That's the way God made us. I fear that the online pseudo-community can temporarily mollify our hunger for a flesh-and-blood fellowship so that we fail to perceive what is lacking in our lives.

Consider also that virtual conversation encourages pretense. It brings out our tendency to "present our best side" when relating to the person on the other side of the computer screen. Chat rooms, discussion boards, and social networks are filled with people pretending to be something that they're not because it's just so easy to do in that kind of setting. How many women are carrying on email conversations right now, fully believing that they are talking with another thirty-something mother of three, when in reality they are spilling their guts to a hairy, fifty-year-old guy using a false identity? This is no place to find reliably authentic community. In some ways you'd be better off sharing a pew with someone. At least then you can see if someone is the right gender.

Every new shift in the culture produces a corresponding

strain of the Christian faith. In our efforts to keep the gospel relevant, we are always reinventing the Church to look like our environment. At some level this must happen as a natural consequence of living as believers in our own time. But some folks are always overdoing it. When the Church simply becomes an extension of the culture, you end up with something that is of no use to any one. It's like salt with no saltiness or a lamp that emits no light. Neither a virtual church, nor a church with no belief in truth, will be able to serve as a light in a world that already looks and thinks that way anyway.

Along the same lines, the world doesn't need us to get cooler haircuts, dress in the latest fashions, listen to hipper music, and spend 12 hours a day hooked to a computer screen.[11] They've already got people doing that. They need to see truly counter-cultural communities of believers speaking the truth to whoever will listen. They need to see the Church expressing the self-giving love of Jesus in practical ways, and they need to feel welcome among us even when we are not welcome among them.

They need to see *Christ in y'all*. That's their hope of glory. When the sons of God are revealed to this broken creation, it reminds us all that better things are coming. God has not left us to die in this condition. He is going to make all things new, and he will give a foretaste of his glory in the Church. Let us never give up on the Church, since that is ultimately what he came

---

[11] Go ahead and do these things if you want. But take care to never become a slave to your culture and its ways. Everything in moderation, you know?

here for. God wants a house, and he wants one *here*. Let's join him in his ambition and never look back.

Afterword

Hopefully, you have seen how the gospel itself, when fully proclaimed, leads to community. The good news is that, in the cross of Christ, we are not only saved from the penalty of our sins. More than that, we are made to participate in the life of Christ himself. We are included in Christ and made one with him, and therefore one with each other as well. By depositing into us his loving, self-giving Spirit, God intends to demonstrate his character for all creation to see.

I cannot prescribe how that Spirit and that character will work itself out in specific, mechanical terms. I can state, however, that God's passion to express himself in this world will never be fully contained within our man-made, traditional forms of worship. Ironically, the freshest, most innovative manifestation of the gospel for today will likely become a stale hindrance to God's work in the future. That's the problem of "wineskins." Living, organic things need an equally living and organic context in which to grow.

So we must content ourselves to imperfectly follow after that Spirit who guides us. We must give ourselves permission to make mistakes along the way, never thinking at any point that "we have arrived." We press on to lay hold of that for which God has laid hold of us. I hope that these few chapters will encourage you to seek his kingdom with all of your heart.

While you're at it, I'd recommend some more reading and searching so that you can benefit from the journeys of other brothers and sisters out there. I've included on the last page a list of books that have helped me along the way. I also have included a list of websites which may connect you with helpful resources online. Happy hunting!

RECOMMENDED READING

Banks, Robert. *Paul's Idea of Community*. Peabody: Hendrickson. 1994.

Barna, George. *Revolution*. Carol Stream: Tyndale. 2005.

Barna, George, and Frank Viola. *Pagan Christianity*. Carol Stream: Tyndale. 2008.

Brother Lawrence. *The Practice of the Presence of God*. New Kinsington: Whitaker House. 1982.

Edwards, Gene. *The Divine Romance*. Carol Stream: Tyndale. 1992.

Fenelon, Francois. *Christian Perfection*. Minneapolis: Bethany House. 1975.

Grubb, Norman. *God Unlimited*. Fort Washington: CLC. 1962.

McVey, Steve. *Grace Walk*. Eugene: Harvest House. 1995.

Tozer, A.W. *The Pursuit of God*. Camp Hill: Christian Publications. 1982.

Viola, Frank. *Reimagining Church*. Colorado Springs: David C. Cook. 2008.

Watchman Nee. *The Normal Christian Life*. Carol Stream: Tyndale. 1977.

Zens, Jon. *A Church Building Every ½ Mile*. Lincoln: Ekklesia Press. 2008.

RESOURCES ONLINE

www.ChristInYall.com - My website.

www.AtlantaSaints.com - The website for my church.

www.ptmin.org - Frank Viola's website.

www.SearchingTogether.org - Jon Zens' writings online.

www.house2house.tv - Tony and Felicity Dale's house church site.

www.JesusCreed.org - Scot McKnight's helpful blog.

www.Seedsowers.com - Publisher of some of my favorite books.

www.ZoeCarnate.com - Super-sized database of useful websites.

www.Barna.org - George Barna's research site.

About the Author

Neil Carter has lived and met in homes with a group of Christians in the Atlanta, Georgia, area since 2000. Originally from Jackson, Mississippi, he graduated from Mississippi College with a Bachelor's Degree in Psychology. He also earned a Master's Degree in Biblical Studies from Reformed Theological Seminary in Jackson. Neil has taught several subjects in both public and private high schools since 1999. Currently, he teaches Literature and History to high school students with special needs.

Neil and his wife April were married in 1996, and together they have four spirited daughters. April is currently a stay-at-home mom who tutors English Composition for a Christian Preparatory school. Both avid writers and readers, they hope to one day get a full night's sleep.

You can contact Neil through his website:
www.ChristInYall.com

Printed in the United States
219996BV00001B/4/P